CLARITY DRIVEN

How to get it right when you can't know it all

For Jo

If you enjoy this, tell everyone! If you hate it, tell me

Jon

JONATHAN COZENS

Clarity Driven: How to get it right when you can't know it all
First published in Great Britain in 2025 by
DAISA PUBLISHING
An imprint of PARTNERSHIP PUBLISHING

A CIP catalogue record for this book is available from the British Library.
ISBN 978-1-915200-72-3

Book cover design by: Partnership Publishing

Book typeset by:
PARTNERSHIP PUBLISHING
North Lincolnshire, United Kingdom

www.partnershippublishing.co.uk
Printed in England

Partnership Publishing is committed to a sustainable future for our business, our readers, and our planet; an organisation dedicated to promoting responsible management of forest resources. This book is made from paper certified by the Forestry Stewardship Council (FSC) an organisation dedicated to promoting responsible management of forest resources.

CLARITY DRIVEN

How to get it right when you can't know it all

JONATHAN COZENS

DEDICATION

For Ann, who bravely kept everything running while I indulged myself in the writing process.

Mum and Dad, whose endless enthusiasm sustained me more than they know.

Mark & Gill, thanks for coffee and brainstorms!

FOREWORD

In an era where data is often referred to as the new oil, the ability to not just collect but also to effectively curate and protect this resource is crucial for any business aiming to thrive. It's an honour to write the foreword for a book that tackles these very issues head-on, penned by someone whose insight I've come to deeply appreciate during our conversations.

The landscape of business intelligence has evolved dramatically over the past three decades or so. When I began my journey as a business founder, the tools and methodologies for decision-making were vastly different from what they are today. Information was scarce, and the process of gathering actionable insights was more art than science. Fast forward to now, and we're in a world where information overload is the new challenge.

This book delves into the art and science of navigating this information-rich environment. It addresses not only how to find the right information but also how to evaluate its relevance and safeguard it from the myriad risks that modern businesses face.

What stands out about this work is its holistic approach. It doesn't just preach the importance of data; it provides a roadmap for transforming data into a strategic asset. The author, with his profound understanding and practical experience, guides the reader through:

- The necessity of information in decision-making: Understanding why quality data is non-negotiable for effective strategy.
- Strategies for information curation: Techniques to sift through the noise and focus on what truly matters.
- Protection and ethical considerations: How to shield your business's lifeblood from cyber threats, competitive espionage, and ethical pitfalls.

Our discussions have been enlightening, revealing Jonathan's depth of knowledge and his ability to connect theoretical insights with practical business outcomes. This book is a testament to his expertise and a valuable resource for anyone from seasoned executives to budding entrepreneurs who understand that in business, knowing what to focus on can be just as important as the focus itself.

Whether you're at the helm of a startup or steering a multinational, the principles laid out in these pages will resonate with the core of what it means to lead in today's fast-paced, information-driven economy. This is not just a book about managing data; it's about empowering decision-makers to make choices that are informed, strategic, and ultimately, transformative.

I look forward to seeing how this book influences its readers, and I am confident it will become an indispensable guide in the toolkit of any serious business strategist.

Dr. David Wolff
Chairman/CEO
The Ethica Group

CONTENTS

INTRODUCTION

INTRODUCTION

Imagine you're starting a long car journey for a much anticipated school reunion at a remote country hotel. You haven't seen your old schoolmates in ages and you're looking forward to a relaxed weekend. You have a destination, and since it's a long journey you have a route planned complete with road names and turn directions. So - with a full fuel tank and a car load of friends (Alice, Bob and Caitlin), you're ready to get going and looking forward to arriving at your destination at the agreed time.

You've only been driving a little while when you see signs for roadworks. Although you get through them in about 15 minutes, you're already behind your expected arrival time. Nobody is that worried as you're all in the same car, and at least everybody with you knows what's going on. Surely being 15 minutes late arriving after a long journey isn't that big a deal, right?

Not much further on, you hit more roadworks, this time with a diversion. At this point you have to trust that the diversion is not long and also clearly marked, as you realise that your map only shows the route you had planned and doesn't include the roads you're currently driving on. As luck would have it, the diversion is easy to navigate but it's not immediately clear where you have rejoined your original route. At this point you know you're further behind schedule but since you're not quite sure where you are, it's not clear by how much.

Finally, you see many flashing lights ahead and realise that there's been an accident. The road has been closed and the police are directing traffic away from the area without further guidance.

This is where a few unfortunate truths become apparent.

Your journey plan started becoming out of date a while ago, and after several unexpected changes you now find yourself driving with no clear idea of where you're going or how to get to where you want to go. Everybody in the car has their own idea of what to do next, but since you're driving it's up to you to decide.

What are your options here?

- Do you stop, try to work out where you are and plan to get back to your original route?
- Do you try to get to your original destination just by dead reckoning?
- Do you abandon your journey plan and try to find somewhere else to go?
- Do you just keep driving and see if you end up somewhere good?

Keep in mind, your plan was to meet some great friends at a known location at an agreed time, and they have no idea that you've been diverted and delayed. Both their weekend and yours will be disrupted if you don't arrive.

Of course, it would help if you had some more information.

If you knew exactly where you were, you could work out whether it was better to try to rejoin your original route or whether to get to your destination directly from your current location.

If you knew how late you were, you could estimate whether a longer journey on faster roads might be more effective than a shorter journey on country lanes.

When it comes down to it, working out what to do next would be a lot easier if your original journey plan had been updated as you went along and new information incorporated.

However, since the best option is not at all clear, you ask your passengers what they think.

Alice is adamant that attempting to navigate direct to your destination is your best option, regardless of how long it takes. Bob thinks that, since finding your way back to the original route has worked so far, that's what you should do. Caitlin feels that the combined view of everyone in the car is bound to be the best option, so she's happy to go with the flow.

I think you'd agree, this is not a great start to your weekend!

At this point, you may well be saying "that's all very well but everybody has a GPS or Sat Nav these days so your example isn't valid" Problem solved, right?

Yes, but it's worth taking a moment to examine why a Sat Nav makes such a fundamental difference. After all, in our example you started with a journey plan and knew what roads to take, so what is it about a Sat Nav that changes everything?

The critical difference is that a Sat Nav is continually and automatically updated with position and timing information.

More to the point, a Sat Nav can get live traffic and road closure updates and so can easily show you the impacts of journey changes to distance and arrival time.

In other words, the difference between a Sat Nav and a paper journey plan is the Sat Nav enables you to make better, more accurate and effective decisions in the context of changing conditions.

Let's apply this example to the world of business.

You'll likely already have realised that the original journey plan above represents the business plan that everyone starts with, which identifies a destination and the actions needed to get there. However, a static business plan is like our set of journey instructions, i.e. it relies on manual updates to remain accurate and therefore useful.

The problem here is that manually updating a plan is complex, takes time and certainly in the context of a small business, can feel like more trouble than it's worth. However, the point of my little story above is to show that an out of date plan is essentially the same as having no plan at all!

So what can we as business owners and leaders do to make sure this scenario never occurs to us?

In this book, I will show how businesses frequently struggle to make effective decisions due to lack of accurate, timely and reliable information. I will describe why this happens as often as it does, and go on to explain how to address the issues it causes.

My intent is to ensure that every business has the best chance to succeed and grow, and isn't arbitrarily held back by avoidable limiting factors.

Who is this book for?

- If you planned for greatness but you're already as busy as you can possibly cope with
- If business growth just looks like more work for you
- If you're drowning in short term decisions
- If your management meetings are spent updating and discussing those updates
- If your business plan lies, unread and neglected in a drawer somewhere

Then this book is for you.

Some of the material I cover applies to larger businesses, but every large business was small once, so the points I make are relevant to new or small ventures planning. Likewise, some of the topics are focused on small business, however larger businesses can still benefit by using this to review their launch experience and how things played out years ago.

MY BUSINESS JOURNEY

To begin, I want to share my own business journey with you, partly to highlight some of the mistakes that could have been avoided had I known then what I know now, but also to shine some light on the inspiration and catalyst for this book.

Let's step back to the summer of 2016. My wife and I had just returned to the UK from 5 blissful years living and working in Australia. I was 54 years old, and despite having gained a wealth of technology and operational management experience over a 35 year career in broadcast TV and corporate IT, I didn't exactly relish the prospect of finding a job that valued my skills more than my age. To say this was a bit of a career crossroads would be putting it mildly!

This was where a long standing idea began to take hold.

On the basis that Ann and I had complementary skill sets and a lot of industrial experience between us, I thought it would be feasible for us to combine our abilities and run our own business.

In the belief that the high failure rate of startups made buying a going concern the most logical choice, finding an existing business felt like our least risky option. Since most of my career to date had been spent in technology functions of one description or another, it seemed like our best chance of success was to buy an IT company and build it up with a view to retiring on the proceeds. After all, everyone in business wants IT services, right?

My intent at the time was to distinguish us from other similarly sized IT companies by leveraging my experience in corporate IT for the benefit of small business customers. Although enterprise technologies don't often work well at small business scale, the logic that makes them useful certainly does. So, my reasoning went, if you engage with me as your IT support partner, I can help you make better technology choices to grow your business since I already have experience of technical operations at scale.

I expected that owners and leaders of SME sized businesses would recognise this as highly or even uniquely valuable, which would make selling technology support services comparatively easy.

I found out pretty quickly and fairly conclusively that my view was not shared by my target market. Nobody cared!

To begin with, this seemed like a sales problem. I knew that we were offering great services, so the value of them should be fairly easy to appreciate. Hoping that it was just an understanding gap, my next move was to re frame these services in the context of relatable business outcomes.

I renamed and re-branded our company as IT For Growth to make it as clear as possible that this was the true role of IT in business, and that our services were directly aligned with our customers' success. Surely I thought, this would do it. This would shine enough light on the value we bring to open up plentiful sales and make us successful.

This led me to an interesting insight. My sales discussions with potential customers had highlighted a widespread mindset that caused them to regard their technology investments as a net cost rather than a net benefit. If that was true then of course they're not going to want to spend money supporting and maintaining systems they didn't really want in the first place!

This was the start of my journey into understanding the 'why' of business technology. After speaking at length with many other businesses, I came to recognise that the business value of technology and its associated support services is simply not clear enough for a non technical audience.

In part, this is because business technology is typically described in the language of 'what' and 'how', in the expectation that the 'why' would be obvious. To put it another way, tech is promoted in terms of what it does and how it does it, i.e. 'features and benefits'. The problem here is that these benefits are necessarily limited in scope to what that system is supposed to do. To be able to assert business wide benefits would require detailed knowledge of how the customer's business actually works, which of course the vendor doesn't have.

What this means is that businesses end up buying all kinds of IT systems that usually do what they claim to do, but turn out not to be much help in improving the overall performance of the enterprise. After being burned once or twice, it's no wonder that business owners tend to cast a slightly jaded eye on the claims made by technology companies!

To illustrate, think about a typical task you use IT for in your business. You may be updating a spreadsheet, creating a report or sending an email for example.

Now consider whether the end result of something as routine as sending an email could also be completed with a typewriter and paper. Obviously, typing a letter and sending it through the mail would be slower than an email but that's not the point. The point is, it could be done without a computer if you had to. You can extend this principle to a huge number of information handling tasks in business.

This is a fundamental point. What it means is we're typically using our very expensive computers as glorified typewriters and fancy filing cabinets! Since computers and their associated systems and services are not exactly cheap, if most of the benefit you're gaining from them could also be achieved with typewriters and paper, then the 'why' of business IT clearly isn't well understood.

This struck me as profound. I had to ask myself whether I could define this mysterious 'why' in a reasonably simple way, such that the business community could start to realise some of the benefits they're currently missing. Although I didn't realise it at the time, this was the start of an entirely new journey, which itself began with a big decision. I realised that I had to sell my IT business.

While much about the future was unclear, one thing was abundantly plain. If I was going to advise businesses on anything even faintly related to technology, I could only do it based on trust. In other words I didn't want my guidance to be interpreted as a sales pitch, and if I was still the owner of a technology services company, that trust could be undermined.

Taking the big leap, I sold IT For Growth in spring 2024 to a more established IT services company to concentrate on developing the ideas that led to this book.

To be absolutely clear, this is not a book about technology, it's entirely about business management. Although my inspiration arose from questions about the role of technology in business, my mission is to explain how effective management of information leads to massively improved business outcomes.

With that said, shall we get started?

THE PROBLEM

WOYBNIYB

There's a phrase that gets bandied around a lot in business, and business owners and leaders tend to nod and smile knowingly when they hear it, because everybody is confident they understand what it means.

The phase is: **"Work on your business, not in your business"** and the concept is that as a business owner or a senior manager, you need to separate yourself from daily repetitive tasks and concentrate on managing.

That sounds clear enough when you first hear it, but it's actually pretty vague. There is a huge number of activities that could conceivably fit within that description, so what does it mean exactly? Is there some kind of objective statement that we can all agree sums this phrase up perfectly?

What I find fascinating are different interpretations of this statement, so when meeting business leaders I like to put the question: "what does working on your business actually mean?" Having asked this simple question many times in different settings from individual meetings to group networking events, I have yet to find two definitions that agree exactly. Try it yourself and see what your results are.

This is actually quite profound. The fact that everybody has their own interpretation means this icon, this celebrated nugget of perceived business wisdom is actually not as well defined as you might think!

Having said that, I have found that regardless of how they are expressed, everybody's answers have one common attribute. They are all examples of decision making.

In other words, working on your business means making decisions.

That's it. No more, no less.

In one sense this is very good news, in that it beautifully clarifies the contribution of business management. Your role as a manager, leader or business owner is to make decisions. Of course, that may not be the only thing you spend your time on, and you may have responsibilities inside the business, carrying out other income generating activity. But making decisions is how you add unique value.

If that were the end of the story, this would be a very short book indeed. However, the gritty reality is that decision-making in business is hard.

- It's frightening - you're aware that every decision may be your last
- It's risky - bad outcomes can be devastating
- It's difficult - how can you make sure your decisions are good ones?

While there are many worthy and well researched academic works written on the subject of decision making, the object of this book is to create a clear, practical, repeatable but most of all useful system for decision making in business.

We'll cover:

- Why the decisions you made before you launch your business are very different to the ones you have to make afterwards
- Why the big decisions are the hardest to make
- Why the hardest decisions are also the most important
- Why the most important decisions are about the distant future, not the present
- Why decisions that were true yesterday can't be relied on today
- Why even small decisions can't be taken in isolation
- How to find the necessary information to minimise the inevitable attendant risks.

We'll start right at the very beginning, with the inspirations and conditions that lead to a business launch.

HOW BUSINESSES START

Have you ever spent time observing someone who's clearly an expert at playing a musical instrument you've never even touched? That inevitable twinge of envy we all feel is most often expressed as 'how do they make it look so easy?' These brilliant and gifted individuals are making the hideously difficult look calm and methodical, but imagining yourself in their shoes seems like some wild flight of fancy.

Making it look easy has a lot of significance in the context of a business launch, because that's the thing most notable by its absence when you're doing it yourself for the first time. The period you spent in planning and decision making felt pretty smooth, in part because the time it took wasn't constrained but mainly because nothing you did could be properly tested. Each decision stayed made, just as you left it.

This is somewhat ironic, because when reading guides on business launches and subsequent operations, it's common to see essential tasks and activities referred to in a rather dispassionate way in terms of lists or check boxes. The expectation seems to be that the launch team, be it a team of one or a team of many, will calmly execute one task after another without huge amounts of excitement and panic!

So when the people most qualified to advise on how best to conduct a business launch give their advice, it's in the context of having done it themselves or guided others many times. In other words, they are making it look easy!

In fact, compared to the maelstrom of the early phase of your business, the planning stage seems like a distant sunny shore indeed.

Now anyone could expect a business launch to be a wild and dynamic time, no huge insight there. So what's my point?

The point is that keeping a business plan up to date is at its most challenging where everything you originally relied on to be true is all being tested at once, in an unstable and rapidly changing environment. If you combine this sudden uncertainty with the emotional impact of potentially being wrong about any number of original expectations, you can see that any reasonable person is going to be very much on the lookout for validation and affirmation.

Taking the musical illustration above, imagine you have spent three months learning to play the piano. You have practised as much as you could in the time available, but on your own or with others of the same skill level. However, you now need to give a public performance in front of 1000 people, none of whom know you, and alongside 9 other experienced pianists. The reward for a good performance is £1000 and the chance to play again tomorrow, but a poor performance means they will set your piano on fire.

Regardless of how well you play, you will try to concentrate on every single aspect of your performance at once while looking out for any sign of encouragement from the audience that they like what you're doing!

Translating this back to our business launch scenario, the other pianists are competitor businesses doing what you're doing, only with more experience. These are the guys and girls making it look easy while you're focused on completing every item on the list of tasks you planned.

You can appreciate this is an intense experience, so what you'll be looking out for as much as anything are clear signs you're actually doing well. By which of course, I mean sales.

Quite apart from cash, sales equal validation. Sales mean that the piano audience that doesn't even know you likes your performance enough to give you money. Sales means everyone who told you that you stood no chance, that you should just get a job, were wrong. You were right and you have money in the bank to prove it.

Let's hear a hooray!

OK, maybe calm down a touch. But it's absolutely true that in the context of a commercially uncertain and emotionally intense launch, sales plays a massively uplifting role as well as a financially valuable one.

However…

In all the excitement that surrounds early success, are the sales you are getting the ones you expected to get? Are you selling what you thought you'd sell, for the amount you wanted, to the people you expected to buy from you?

Let's not forget, sales are the end result of a number of other activities, each of which had some element of planning around it. To put it another way, even if your raw income is about what you projected, how much of your plan does that validate? The only way you will know for sure is by checking all the elements of your plan and confirming that all of your estimates are still accurate.

If it turns out that there are discrepancies between what your plan said would be true, and what turns out to be actually true, then your logical next step is to examine those discrepancies and try to establish their separate root causes. If that doesn't sound like a whole heap of fun, you'd probably be right. After all, you're making money so the details can't be all that important, right?

I'm sure you can see where this is going. Even at this early stage, your business plan is at risk of becoming out of date and therefore effectively useless. It's quite a short step from here to the plan being disregarded altogether as being more trouble than its worth and consigned to the desk drawer of obscurity. If you expected most of the difficulty relating to keeping a business plan up to date to arise later in the business journey when overall complexity and transaction volumes are both higher, think again.

So why bother at all?

If an up to date business plan is such a hard thing to maintain, and may not be essential to success, do we really need to bother with one? Can't we just wing it? This is where we refer back to the statistical evidence from the business community. Although a continually accurate plan is not essential to every business in every case, there is overwhelming evidence that your chances of both survival and success are substantially higher if you have one.

BUSINESS PLANS ARE NOT USEFUL

I want to talk about business plans and the expectations that surround them. There is a major problem with business plans that in my view is not sufficiently recognised at small to medium business scale.

If you talk to any business coach or mentor, any lender or investor and they will inevitably ask you about your business plan. In their view, to not have one is seen as the gravest crime, the grossest dereliction for a business leader or entrepreneur.

The implication here is that having a business plan is an absolute requirement, from which you might expect that a business plan is your magical key to success. If that were true, then there would be an almost 100% correlation between having a plan and business success. Let's test that assertion.

Some example statistical evidence from the USA shows the following:

SBA and SCORE: According to SCORE, a nonprofit organisation associated with the SBA, businesses that have a written business plan are more likely to succeed. SCORE reports that businesses with a plan grow 30% faster than those without one, and 71% of fast-growing companies have business plans.

Journal of Small Business Management (2007): This study found that firms that completed business plans were more likely to become profitable and achieve their goals. The study indicated that planning was positively correlated with the success of small businesses.

Palo Alto Software Survey: This survey found that companies with a business plan were twice as likely to secure capital and subsequently grow, compared to those without a plan. The survey indicated that 64% of businesses with a plan grew their business, compared to 43% of those without a plan.

Cox Business Survey (2016): This survey highlighted that businesses with a business plan are more likely to secure funding and manage their cash flow effectively, reducing the risk of failure.

While these stats indicate a clear correlation between having a plan and success, the fact that the number isn't even close to 100% in every case indicates that having a business plan isn't a guarantee of a good commercial outcome nor is the absence of a plan a certain path to failure.

So what's missing here? Let's ask another organisation with a vested interest in good outcomes, the military.

Dwight D. Eisenhower, a man particularly noted for his planning ability is recorded as saying "Plans are worthless, but planning is everything"

This point was also made by Helmuth von Moltke the Elder who, slightly paraphrased, said "No plan survives first contact with the enemy"

Even Mike Tyson had his own take on this, and famously said "Everyone has a plan 'till they get punched in the mouth."

In other words, and evidenced by people who knew what they were talking about, however carefully you build your plan it won't be accurate for very long.

Recall the example of our friends on their car journey from the introduction. Their plan was accurate in every detail but each time their journey deviated from the plan, it became less and less useful to the point where it was no use at all. To put it as simply as possible, a plan that has deviated from reality even a little has zero value. Unless you count the ability to say "we're no longer sure what's going on" as value. I didn't think so!

So if having a plan, even a good plan, doesn't guarantee a desired result, what does?

The crucial difference is that a plan is a static document. It incorporates intentions, information and decisions that were all believed true at a specific point in time. However, the real world is not so accommodating as to stay perfectly still just because your plan reflects it doing so.

What does all this look like in the business world?

Let's imagine an example small business that launched a year or so ago. They went through the usual business planning process before they launched, and created a comprehensive document that contained all the marketing, sales, operations and financial figures you would expect. Having built this entirely adequate plan, they launched the business and started trading.

What do you think happened after their planning numbers became a little out of date?

These are highly motivated people with most of the information they need rather than all of it, so naturally they pressed on in search of wealth and wonder. Equally naturally, and as I have seen in many cases, their originally accurate business plan becomes increasingly obsolete to the point where it gets relegated to a desk drawer, never to see the light of day again until requested by their coach or bank manager. The resulting discussion is not particularly comfortable for either side!

Now you're probably saying to yourself (or possibly even screaming at this very page) that the answer is obvious. Just keep the plan up to date and everything will be all right.

If only it were that simple.

There are two issues to contend with here. The first and arguably most trivial is that updating a plan is a complex, delicate and labour intensive activity that can only be completed by the busiest people in the organisation, the management team. These people (i.e. you) have a huge variety of calls on their time, and dedicating an unknown amount of that to updating a document they have already lost some degree of faith in is not an enticing prospect.

The second and massively more significant issue is that a plan is supposed to be a useful tool for predicting the future. If it's only useful in that regard just after it's been updated then overall it's not very useful at all. Worse still, if the update activity then reveals a reality that is materially different to what was expected, then some profound decisions need to be made, and quickly. Regardless of how necessary it is, how many times do you truly want to go through that process?

The more frequently you update your plan in the interests of accuracy and currency, the more time you spend doing that instead of running the business. What all this ends up with, is in effect you working for the plan that's supposed to be working for you!

So what to do? If planning is crucial but static plans are not useful, how do we ensure success in business?

BUSINESS PLANS

WHAT IS A BUSINESS PLAN?

If you were to ask a room full of business people a simple question 'what is a business plan?', you would hear many contributions along the lines of:

- An executive summary
- A financial statement
- A marketing plan
- A sales plan
- A hiring strategy and org chart
- A health and safety plan

...and so on.

I'd like to draw a very important distinction here.

Worthwhile and valuable as the above items are, they only describe what a business plan contains, not what it is.

At its core, a business plan is simply a set of decisions with a corresponding set of assumptions. That's it. That may seem like a provocative statement so let me show you what I mean.

Going into business is a decision. It's a decision you made or possibly have yet to make, but let's be honest here, as decisions go it's a biggie! Whatever your motivation for starting a business, it's not going to happen by accident. There are many good reasons not to go into business for yourself so it's crucial to recognise that if you do decide to push ahead and launch a business, everything after this point will happen in the context of this original decision.

Let's break this down a bit.

Although there are as many reasons for launching a business as there are people prepared to do it, they all have one thing in common. They describe a world you would like to see.

This ideal world could be directly for your benefit or it could revolve around a benefit to others. For example, you could say "I want to carry on activity 'x' to make myself rich" Or you could say "I want to carry on activity 'y' because the world needs that activity".

OK, nothing too radical so far, right? We've just captured the vision for your business, i.e. a simple statement that describes the world you would like to see.

However, there is a big piece missing here, and that is the corresponding assumptions that accompany your decision.

What do I mean by corresponding assumptions?

Decisions can't be made completely and utterly in isolation, they are always made based on one or more assumptions which we both believe and depend on to be true. Some of these assumptions are so extraordinarily well tested, we take them for granted which means they're not obvious. For example, when we go to sleep at the end of the day we assume the sun will come up in the morning, and we make our plans for tomorrow in the expectation that this is absolutely going to happen.

Likewise, we also assume that when we go to sleep, we assume we're not going to unexpectedly wake up one million pounds richer (or poorer!) and again we make our plans for tomorrow on that basis.

The sun coming up tomorrow, and not waking up magically more wealthy are just examples of a whole set of assumptions we make that are similarly well tested, and this set can be called 'tomorrow looks very much like today'. We spend our lives immersed in this continuity, to the extent that we depend on it to make decisions.

Think back to the night before a major exam or a big business event or some other life changing experience. You'll remember the sense of tension, whether it was excitement or worry. That feeling was due, at least in part, to the knowledge that tomorrow would be very different to today and since this is actually quite a rare occurrence we're not well equipped to cope with it.

The flip side is, knowing that tomorrow will look very much like today is a very handy tool for making decisions, since it limits the number of variables you need to take into account, and gives you the sense that your predictions are being made in isolation.

But there's a couple of problems here, and they're pretty significant.

Firstly, tomorrow being the same as today is only true up to a point. In reality, tomorrow is only mostly like today, not exactly the same. While the difference may be small, it's still there. This means that the day after tomorrow is even less like today and the day after that even less than that and so on. The point here is that this expectation of continuity is only valid over very short timescales. So if you want to make longer term decisions in the same way, i.e. expecting that next year will look like this year, your chances of being correct are substantially lower since so much can happen in that time.

Next, although this day to day continuity is pretty reliable, it's not 100% reliable. There have been pivotal moments in history when extraordinary events have happened in the blink of an eye and all of a sudden we have no idea what tomorrow looks like. If you'd made a complex but well researched 12 month plan in mid 2019, at least part of that plan would have been based on the assumption that only a limited amount of change would happen in the coming year. As we all found out the hard way, such an apparently safe assumption would turn out to be completely and utterly wrong!

It's worth emphasising that this isn't a problem in itself. In general change happens fairly slowly and this slow rate of change allows us to make short term decisions in an efficient way. However, when making plans of any duration, it's important to keep in mind that there are already a number of built in assumptions that could be wrong, so take some time to ask yourself what they might be and what you would do if things don't turn out as you might reasonably expect.

So that's an initial set of assumptions to keep in mind, are there any more?

Oh yes.

The next set is 'assumptions you want to be true', and these are crucial. They are much easier to spot, but in a way much harder to test because you are already invested in them being correct. For each major decision you make, there will be a principal corresponding assumption, and it's this that needs the most careful scrutiny.

So what could this principal corresponding assumption be for your vision statement? What qualifying attribute does your better world need? Let's take an example:

Suppose I said "I believe that too many snails get stepped on where people walk. I'd like to see a world where snails had better safety and a lower risk of being squashed. They should have Hi Viz paint on their shells and little crash helmets to wear". You would very likely think 'but that's just a stupid vision Jon, why would anybody bother to do that?'. In other words, nobody else is ever going to care. It doesn't matter how passionate I am about snail safety, nobody is ever going to be invested in it with me.

The point I am making here is that we have just isolated the supporting assumption for my business vision. For every 'this is the world I want to see' decision, the principal corresponding assumption is; 'and enough other people will see things the same way as me that I can make a business out of it'. If nobody else cares about my vision, it makes no difference how strongly I feel about it, or how good I am at making it real, there won't be a viable business for me. Alternatively, if your vision of a better world resonates strongly with a large number of other people, then your chances of commercial success just went from 'dubious' to 'highly likely'.

This is the first test of any business dream and the first example of a business plan being a set of decisions with corresponding assumptions.

Moving on.

After your vision statement has been partnered up with its leading assumption, it's time to look at your business mission or 'what we are going to do to achieve to this ideal world'. Let's go back to our snail safety enterprise.

Let's assume that I have somehow managed to get enough potential customers engaged in my 'Hi Viz for snails' vision to support a business. How am I going to achieve this fabulously desirable outcome? As mentioned above, I could set up a production line making tiny crash helmets with cute little chin straps, and start developing a weatherproof high visibility paint suitable for snail

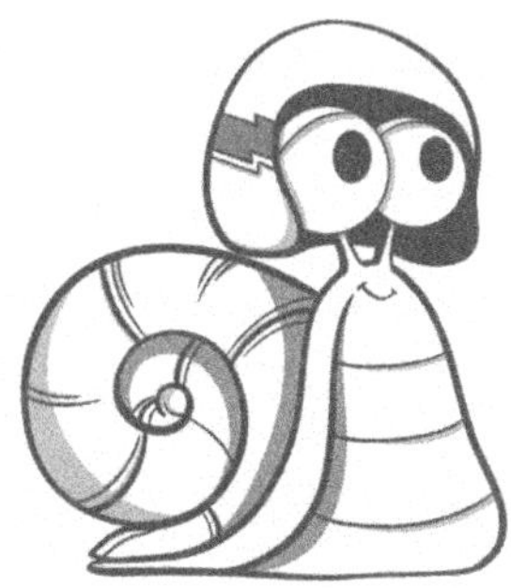

shells. (As an aside, while I'm not sure whether snails actually have chins, I hope we can all agree "The Cute Snail Chin Straps" would be a great name for a band).

Of course, alongside all the other skills essential for business such as marketing and finance, my team really ought to have at least some expertise in plastics and paint chemistry. If they don't have those, then my business mission is at great risk. In other words, the corresponding assumption that goes along with your business mission is 'and we are the right people to achieve it'. If your team doesn't have enough of the specific skills, experience and attitudes to achieve your aim, then your chances of success are pretty dismal.

As you dig further into your business plan, you'll start adding additional decisions around marketing, sales, service, finance and so on. It's crucial to recognise that each of these subsidiary decisions exist within the context of and support the bigger, broader decisions above them.

If we take the example of your marketing plan, all your marketing activities are based on the understanding that you know who your market is, where to find them and how to motivate them to buy from you. That in itself is an assumption, but it exists within the very first assumption you made when you decided that there were enough people out there to make a viable customer base.

So your marketing plan makes sense in the context of your business mission but would be different for anyone else's business.

We can now see a clear pattern building up. Every statement in your plan is a decision, and every decision has a primary corresponding assumption. Let's use a thumbnail sketch to illustrate.

STAGE	DECISION	ASSUMPTION
Vision statement	There's a better world I'd like to see and I'm going to make it happen	Other people see it too, enough to make a business
Mission statement	This is what we're going to do to achieve it	We are the right people with all the necessary attributes
Marketing plan	This is what we're going to do to reach our audience	Our vision is correct
Sales plan	This is what we're going to do to turn marketing output into new business	Our marketing plan is correct
Financial plan	This is how we're going to turn all this business activity into cash	Our sales plan is correct

There are a couple of absolutely critical points to take on board here. Firstly and most importantly, you need to be both clear and honest with yourself about your assumptions.

Why might that be an issue?

It's because our assumptions are also all the reasons why our fondly imagined, desperately desired business dreams might not work. On that basis, it's emotionally very hard to subject our dreams to real scrutiny. After all, having that dream in your heart can sustain you through difficulty and adversity through sheer desire to see it come true. Bringing the light of investigation to bear may show you that one or more of your essential assumptions isn't actually true which means all the ones below it are not true either. If it turns out that your vision is not sustainable, as in our case where precisely nobody cares about snail safety, then the dreams we invested so much passion in are completely worthless.

It's no wonder that there's a strong temptation to either express your assumptions in limited terms, for example "I know 3 other people who acknowledge that snail safety might be a thing, therefore I'm going to interpret that as a worldwide market for snail safety products", or worse still simply not examine them at all. To fall victim to this is to risk everything.

Secondly, as we've already seen, our assumptions have a hierarchy. Each one depends on the accuracy of its predecessor. This significance of this should not be underestimated. It means that the first and biggest assumptions should be subjected to the harshest examination as they will have the biggest impact. To put it another way, the smallest decisions that affect individual actions and tasks will be based on multiple layers of assumptions. If you've ever been given a task to complete at work and thought "why are we even doing this, doesn't anybody know what's going on?" it's worth bearing in mind that the justification for that task is likely to be the product of a whole nest of assumptions, any one of which could steer you in the wrong direction if it was insufficiently tested or just plain incorrect.

So we have highlighted the degree to which a business plan intended to reflect reality is based on assumptions we have to make but over which we have no control.

So how are we going to fix this? What do we need to test our assumptions?

ASSUMPTIONS VS. SUPPORTING DATA

We've shown how business plans are, at their core, simply a set of decisions supported by a corresponding set of assumptions. Whether those decisions are good ones or not depends entirely on how well those assumptions stand up to scrutiny.

What does that scrutiny look like? What information could we bring to bear to show whether our initial set of assumptions are true?

- Personal experience
- Shared experience
- External research
- Operational data

Let's start with personal experience and its strengths and weaknesses.

Without meaning to be glib, where personal experience really scores is it's personal. This means that the sum of everything you have learned in life and in business is brought to bear when considering whether a statement or decision is true or not. Since your set of experiences is unique to you, it means you have the ability to examine information that might be widely available and apply valuable new insight or perspective to it.

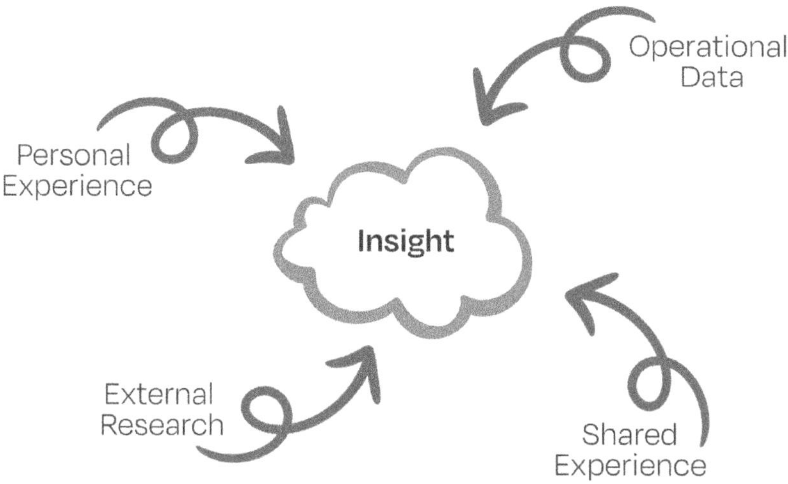

This is how businesses start based on a good idea. We might even say 'simply' a good idea but in truth it's not simple at all. What happens is that the unique combination of that person's experiences, skills and attitudes meant they were able to see an opportunity where nobody else had. While they may feel that whatever they spotted was an opportunity just lying out in the open, almost inevitable, to everyone else it will look like a dazzling intellectual leap into the unknown. Of course, looking back the popular opinion might be "well it was bound to happen sooner or later" but that's missing the point. What's important is that they saw it before anyone else.

It's a good start to be sure, but we're not off to the races just yet. You see, the ability to interpret information in a unique way is helpful but not the same as comprehensive analysis. There's a temptation to assume that insight is the same as infallibility, simply because it makes us feel good. Let's face it, who wouldn't enjoy the feeling of being right, against the odds and when everybody thinks you're wrong.

So on the strength of 'I realised a thing that nobody else has', your first assumption is likely to be 'there's enough potential in it to create a business'. Your corresponding first test of that assumption will probably be 'and my 10 years of experience gives me a high degree of confidence that I'm right' which is comforting and feels like confirmation but you still haven't applied any independent input here such as numerical supporting data or market research.

The thing to bear in mind is you may be right but only partially right. In other words, your poorly tested assumption behaves like one that was thoroughly checked, to the extent that your business launches and makes some early sales. The issue is that early income strongly suggests that your testing was complete and your assumption needs no further examination. So when sales dry up or some other effect happens that relied on your first and most profound assumptions being true, you find yourself very much adrift. Remember, it's not clear what's going on as you believed you checked everything you're relying on yourself.

In case it isn't already clear, this won't be your very best week...

So there's a risk there, but so long as you're aware of it and are as honest with yourself as you can be and subject eeverything you want to be true to the most intense scrutiny, then your chances of success will be as good as they can be.

So if relying on one person's insight to test business assumptions ends up bundling a lot of risk in one place, why don't you spread that risk by applying the expertise of several experienced people? Instead of launching a business off the back of one person's great idea, why not subject all the assumptions around that idea to the input of a whole team? Surely their combined expertise and experience will give you the robust oversight needed?

Well yes, but then again not quite. The attendant risk here is that many opinions versus one doesn't actually apply any more concrete information than you had before. What it does do however is add a reinforcing element to assumptions that several people are now personally invested in. If you feel intuitively that a certain statement is correct, and someone else agrees with you, you end up believing that statement now has a lot more strength behind it when in fact it may only have a little more. As per our previous example, if a business is launched based on the subjective assumption checking of a team rather than an individual, then when things go wrong it's going to be even harder to work out what was missed.

How can we apply more structure to our testing? After all, everything we're trying to achieve relies on our decisions being good ones.

If you're setting out in an established business sector or vertical, then the obvious way of doing this is to carry out market or industrial research. On the basis that there are many more established types of business than entirely new ones, then there will be a lot of information available on industry trends or how specific businesses were affected by them. Some of this information is in the public domain, some of it you will have to pay for. You may even want to commission someone to carry out this activity for you. Whatever options you choose, the point of the exercise hasn't changed. You have made some decisions based on certain assumptions. You need independently verified information to test the extent to which these assumptions are true.

So with appropriate care, attention to detail and supporting third party research, all your decisions are now sufficiently well supported that you can launch. Well done!

So 'well done' didn't last more than a day or so. The champagne is long gone and the last slice of an extravagantly large cake is quietly drying out in the fridge before being consigned to the bin. Your launch is over and now you're just another business trying to stay alive and grow. In terms of decision making, you now have a whole new set of challenges to face, the first of which is time pressure.

Assuming you have only been in business for a short time, one of the luxuries you had before launch but maybe didn't spot was time and plenty of it. In other words, if you didn't have some piece of information you needed, you had at least some control over your launch timetable and could delay it if needed to complete all your planning. That was then, this is now.

Customers are waiting, suppliers are supplying, business operations have a pace of their own and they won't be denied. This means all your decisions have to be made to a quality standard you have already set for yourself but in an immovable time frame. Stressful though that is, it's only the context to a notably harder proposition. You see, all the external data and business information you acquired and applied before launch, was needed to support assumptions you had to make but had no other way of testing. What has suddenly changed is that your decisions and assumptions now need to be tested with your own business data. You've moved beyond information about businesses like yours in the general case and you're suddenly needing high quality data about your own, unique business.

Why is this a problem? Well we'll examine that in considerable detail as we go further through this book. However possibly the biggest difference between you and another business that has been trading a while is accumulated data. Specifically, they have plenty and you have none.

It's worth considering why this is such a big deal as, in the fizz and bubble of the early weeks and months of a new venture, understanding how closely you're tracking against plan is vital but easy to miss.

BUSINESS DATA

DATA - THE LIFEBLOOD OF YOUR BUSINESS

Having established that accurate, up to date information is key to testing the assumptions you make, let's look at it in a little more detail. How is it created and most importantly, why?

To begin with, I should draw an important distinction. There are two kinds of information or data to work with, and they are useful in different ways.

We'll start with the information that describes what's happening right now. This is the kind of information that shows up to the minute marketing and sales activity, your supplier and service delivery status, your current account balance and your tax liability. If you want an operational snapshot of one specific area or even your whole business, then this is the data you look for.

It's important to understand that data of this type is created everywhere in your business, it's a natural consequence of business operations. However, just because it's created, it doesn't necessarily mean it's stored. And just because it's stored, it doesn't mean it's accessible.

Common data locations in small to medium business;

- Enterprise software
- Spreadsheets and other files
- Paper records

- Wallboards
- Noticeboards
- Post it notes
- People's heads

Since you now know why you might need to use this data, you can probably already see that some of these locations might be just a tad less suitable than others. We'll look at how digital data is stored, managed, displayed and made useful in a later section, for now it's important to recognise there may be crucial decision making data in the business that isn't digital, in other words that you simply can't access from your computer.

If a decision you need to make requires the latest operational information, but that information has been captured on a giant marker board in another office, then you're going to have to ask someone for it or get up and go see yourself. Neither of these options are ideal. The same goes for paper sheets pinned to notice boards and sticky notes on people's monitors.

There is a requirement on business leaders to understand how their data is being captured, and making sure it's available for management purposes as well as operational ones. Please note - these two requirements may have some conflict! What do I mean by conflict? For example, if you have traditionally captured one kind of information on a marker board, say shipping or project status where many people need to see a visual representation of complex data, then demanding that information now gets captured in computer software for management purposes is going to have a negative impact as well as a positive one. People who are used to working a certain way may feel that impact quite keenly!

However, operational 'up to the minute' data is not our only source of decision making fuel. Let's take a sales based example.

Find your last set of sales data, then ask yourself the following questions:

- What did you sell?
- Who did you sell it to?
- What was the sales price?
- What was the markup?

All fairly simple stuff, right? The answers you're looking for are there. Now with that data already in front of you, can you tell:

- How did last month's sales compare to the previous month?
- How about the same month last year?
- What was the proportion of repeat sales compared to net new sales?
- Who are your best returning customers?
- Are there any seasonal or other cyclical sales trends?
- What does next month's sales look like based if the last 3 months trends continue?
- What about the next 2 quarters?

Still too obvious? How about:

- What effect did the last change you made to your marketing activity have on the timing of your next hire?

Wait, why would you care about that?

Consider that marketing generates sales, sales grow the business and a growing business is likely to need more people. If your business plan shows a growing head count and a time frame for each new hire, then your hiring schedule will be affected to some extent by your marketing activity. Since hiring people can easily take months, it might be helpful to be able to more accurately predict when you'll need that extra head.

To to answer these kinds of more comprehensive questions, you need to explore the relationships between multiple sets of data in order to reach a conclusion. To be clear, those relationships become data sets themselves!

In other words, the result of comparing data sets actually creates data of its own. You could think of it as data about data. The technical term for this newly created information is metadata, and it's the critical ingredient for forward looking, evidence based decision making.

So we have two completely different categories of information to work with. How do we make them useful? To begin with, it's worth reviewing what we're trying to test or prove. This breaks down into a couple of categories:

1) The assumptions we have already made. Here we're looking in the rear view mirror and even though management focus tends towards the future, it's important to do so. Why would that be? Because if testing our assumptions before we make decisions is a good idea, testing them again afterwards is an even better one. By comparing what we thought would happen with what actually happened, we have the opportunity to reassess the rigour and robustness of those original assumptions.

This is solid gold when it comes to making new, forward looking decisions. If we can show how accurate (or otherwise!) our original assumptions were, it boosts the authority of all the new ones we need to make as we grow the business.

2) The new decisions we've made in the light of real world experience. As highlighted previously, the one thing that's guaranteed is things won't turn out quite the way we expected. The differences may be large or small, but the important point is to recognise them, and incorporate into a revised plan.

If we take the example above regarding short term sales data, while we're retrospectively examining discrepancies, we're also adapting to the updated conditions and adopting them in our business operations.

Having said all that, of course what we're really interested in is making decisions about the future. That's where the growth and the profit lie.

CUSTOMER JOURNEY

So we know that operational and financial data enables you to both run your business effectively and helps you actively remove some of the risks around growth.

Let's look again at where that data might come from.

A really helpful model for thinking about business data is your customer journey, i.e. every interaction a customer has with you on their path from first hearing about your business to completing a purchase and beyond. Quite apart from its logical flow, one reason this model is so helpful is it clearly illustrates how the information you accumulate reveals more and more about your customers, their wants and needs and their buying habits.

For example, if a potential customer signs up to your web site or newsletter, all you know about them is they are aware of your business, an email address and possibly their name. However, by the time they have bought from you several times, you will understand a lot more about who they are, where they live, what aspects or attributes of your product or service are most important to them. In the context of decision making, this is solid gold.

You could visualise accumulating customer insight as a snowball growing larger and larger as it rolls downhill. By the time reaches the bottom of the hill, your tiny snowball of insight could be massive. For the curious, The Tiny Snowballs of Insight is definitely my new band name.

The benefits keep coming. The more you know about the customers you have, the more confidence you can place in assumptions about customers you don't have yet. These might be people that you haven't been able to reach or existing customers who might be interested in new products or services.

Let's look at a generic version of the customer journey to illustrate.

Although there are fundamental differences between B2B and B2C businesses, as well as between service based and product based enterprises, we're interested in what makes businesses the same rather than what makes them different. A simplified customer journey model will therefore come out as 'one size fits none' but the principle is valid regardless.

You can see from the diagram below that there is a lot of information you could collect from each step of an example customer journey. Think about how your own business operates and what data you could capture.

Moving on, finding the data you have is comparatively easy compared to the data you don't have. What information would help you make better decisions? What information WOULD you create if you could create anything?

Look at the data you have and think about out how to discover what doesn't exist yet.

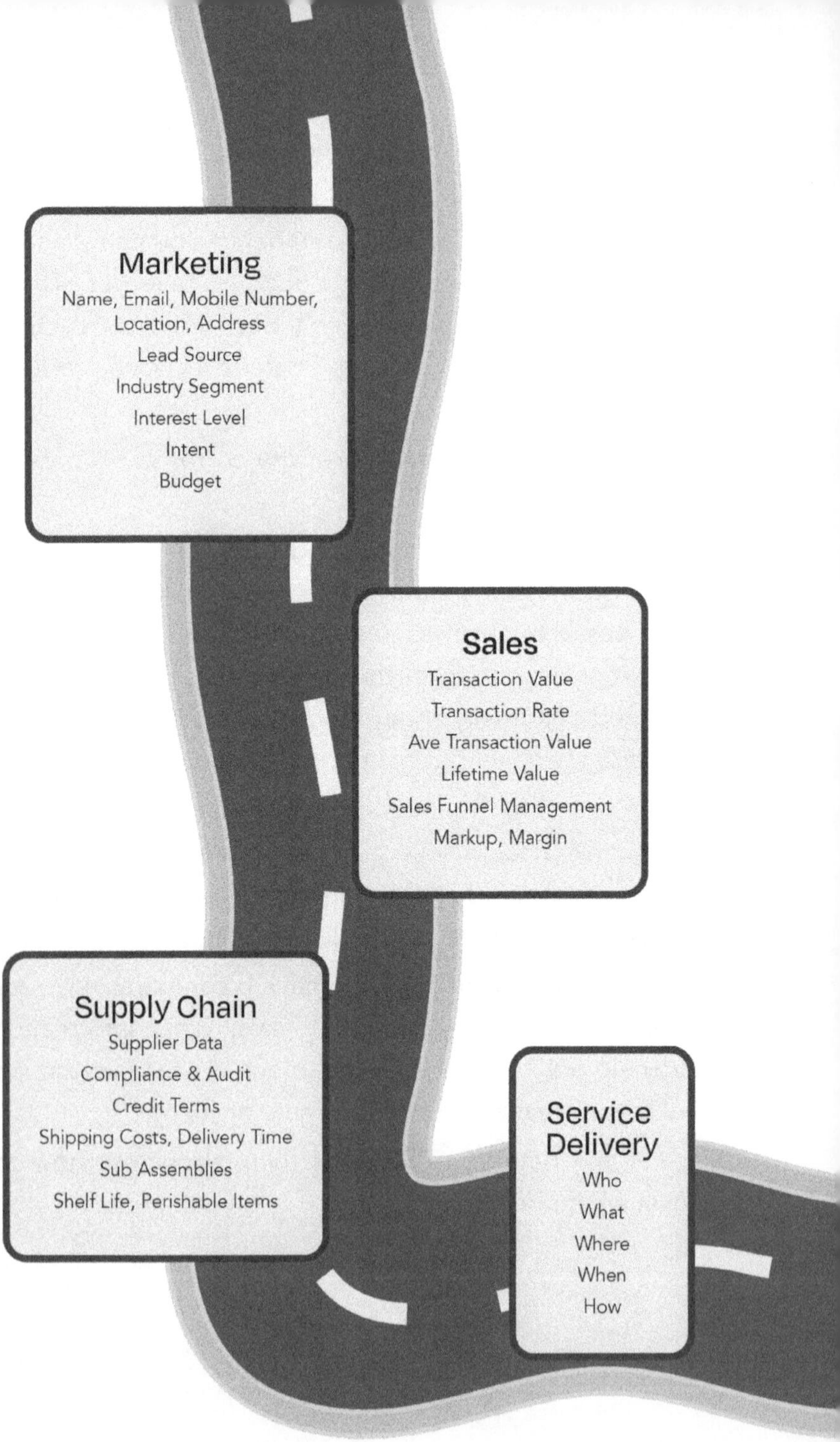
Marketing
Name, Email, Mobile Number, Location, Address
Lead Source
Industry Segment
Interest Level
Intent
Budget
Sales
Transaction Value
Transaction Rate
Ave Transaction Value
Lifetime Value
Sales Funnel Management
Markup, Margin
Supply Chain
Supplier Data
Compliance & Audit
Credit Terms
Shipping Costs, Delivery Time
Sub Assemblies
Shelf Life, Perishable Items
Service Delivery
Who
What
Where
When
How

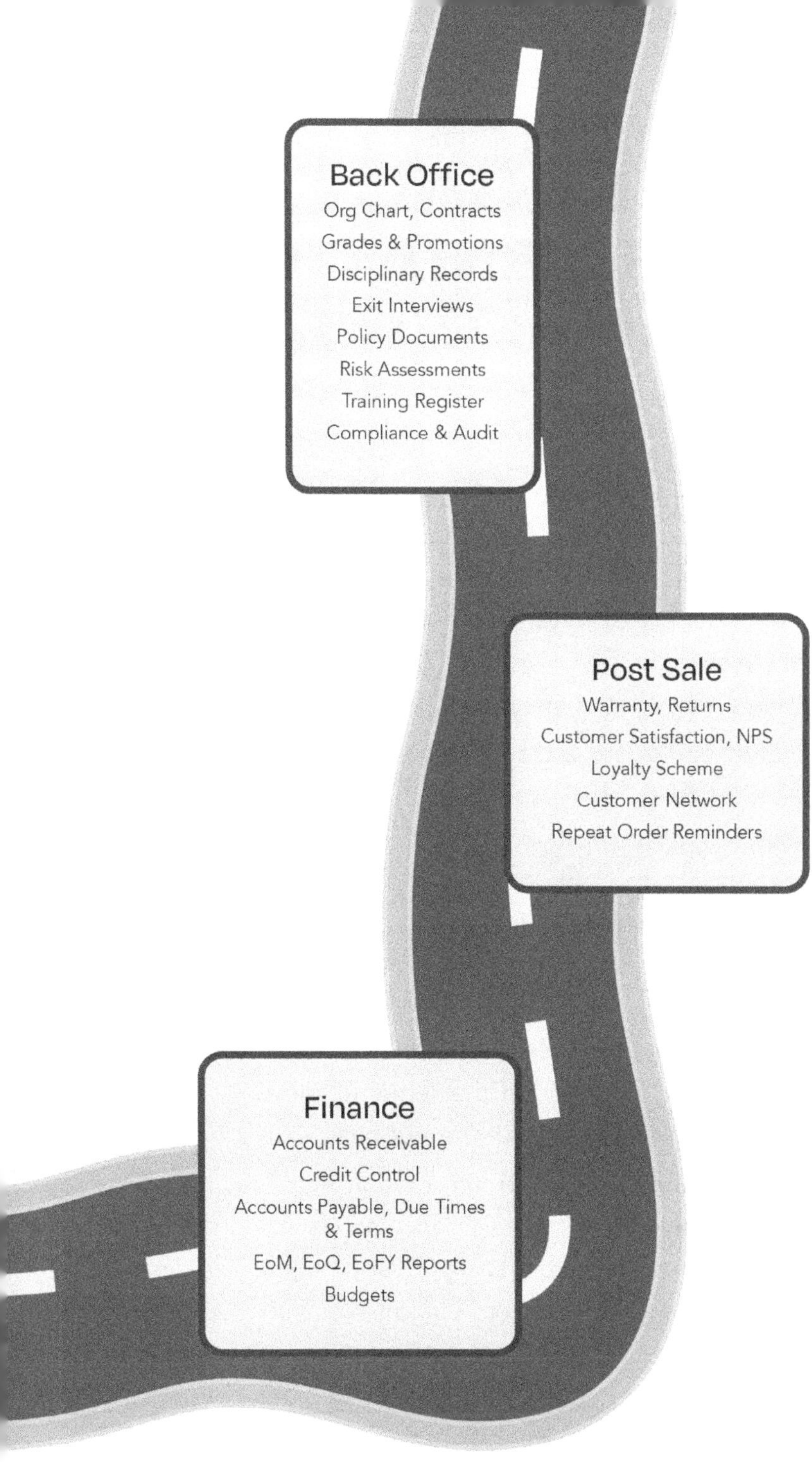
Back Office
Org Chart, Contracts
Grades & Promotions
Disciplinary Records
Exit Interviews
Policy Documents
Risk Assessments
Training Register
Compliance & Audit
Post Sale
Warranty, Returns
Customer Satisfaction, NPS
Loyalty Scheme
Customer Network
Repeat Order Reminders
Finance
Accounts Receivable
Credit Control
Accounts Payable, Due Times & Terms
EoM, EoQ, EoFY Reports
Budgets

LEGACY INFORMATION MANAGEMENT

We're comfortable now with the idea of data driven or evidence based decision making, and the utility of business data as decision making fuel. That's fine as far as it goes, but having established that this data is both created and stored in a wide variety of ways, how are we going to start making what we have, useful?

We need to start with anything that isn't digital. As we indicated earlier, it's a good idea to look at your business and understand where things such as sticky notes, notice boards, marker boards and similar are in use as it's possible they represent the only copy of the information they hold. You will often find this in local or personal workarounds for systems such as business software that are poorly understood, too complex or just not fit for purpose. Since people are resourceful creatures, they will typically create a 'just this once' workaround that ends up becoming the de facto process for that area of the business.

This is significant because information that lives on paper or other non digital storage has serious shortcomings. Firstly, it can't be shared easily. Even if copies are made, the copies have no further relationship with the original data they were created from. If the original data changes, any copies will not reflect that so any decisions made using them will automatically be wrong. Secondly, copying printed information is vulnerable to errors regardless of whether the copying process is manual such as typing or by other means such as photocopying. A lower case letter l can easily be mistaken for the number 1, o and 0 (oh and zero respectively) have the same problem and there are other examples to contend with.

It's worth adding some extra context around large format dry wipe marker boards, as these can be operationally very useful and are therefore hard to abandon. The reason they are useful is they can hold a lot of information in a single place, and they make all that information visible to a large number of people at once. In locations such as call centres or factory floors, being able to see large amounts of operational data at a glance (more on this later) is very helpful.

However, here's the thing to keep in mind when thinking about marker boards. The information on them is exceedingly fragile. By fragile, I mean that a careless (or malicious!) wipe can destroy significant amounts of critical data. If someone were to stumble against a marker board and their sleeve brushed across it, you could find that you're suddenly missing this week's order status or sales pipeline!

Now you may be thinking that's not likely in your business environment, but point is whether it could ever happen, rather than how unlikely it is. Recovering from such an event could be a huge effort, particularly if the lost data was the only copy. Even if the board data is a copy of paper records held elsewhere, then you may have protected the original data but at the expense of the time taken to duplicate it onto a board, combined with the likely copying errors highlighted above.

So where you find non digital record keeping or display, you need to make sure that information is captured and stored in a manner that - at the very least - makes copying and sharing instant, error free and with no risk of multiple versions existing.

KPIS AND COMPLIANCE

If I showed you a whole page of fingerprints, and asked you what you were looking at, you would quite reasonably say 'some fingerprints'. In other words, you are describing what you are seeing as a class of things, even though each of them is as unique as a er, fingerprint.

If I then showed you a single fingerprint and asked you what you were looking at, you would probably say 'someone's fingerprint'.

This is interesting. When thinking about a class of unique items, we tend to describe them in terms of what makes them similar. However when looking at a single example from that class, we're more inclined to focus on the attributes that makes it unique. The psychology behind this is beyond the scope of this book, however it does illustrate an important point. It is entirely possible for something to be unique at the same time as fitting into a broad class of similar objects with common attributes.

This is meaningful to us because it is not only possible but more or less inevitable for a business to be unique and yet not that special at the same time. When you talk to a business owner, all you'll hear about is what makes their venture individual and different. This is quite normal, after all a key part of competition is differentiation so it makes sense to emphasise this when describing what you do.

At the same time, the things that make businesses the same are just as significant. For all businesses, money comes in, money goes out. People do worthwhile work and goods and services are created and delivered.

In this context, I want to look at Key Performance Indicators or KPIs.

The intent behind KPIs is to identify a few critical parameters that combined, act as a meaningful health check for your business. As a health check, they should be presented in an easy to understand form, with some clear way of highlighting when any of them has strayed beyond an expected range.

How many is a few? What should 'healthy' include? How often should they be updated?

My rule of thumb around KPI quantity is 'no more than can be easily seen on a laptop screen' and understood in a single glance. So we need to be thinking about 6 - 8 parameters.

Specifically, what KPIs should we choose? This is extra important to us now that we have identified and harnessed large amounts of data about our business. There's a risk of drowning in information and running into decision paralysis through an overabundance of data. How should we prioritise what to include?

The answer comes in two parts. To begin with, there are KPIs that are common to most businesses, such as sales or financial performance. These are pivotal numbers and really shouldn't be ignored. That's fine as far as it goes, but relying on the same set of KPIs that everyone else uses will inevitably drive your business to look like, yes you guessed it, everyone else's. So despite talking with passion and conviction about how special your business is, the evidence will show that that's just so much hot air!

So a balance must be found. The day to day, month to month (or minute to minute!) indicators of business performance need to reflect uniqueness as well as commonality. OK, but what should your 'we're unique' of KPIs look like? What information is important here?

To answer this second part, we need to go right back to the beginning of your business journey.

Before you launched, when you had your original vision and a sense of mission, the thought foremost in your mind was 'we can't fail, because…' This was why you believed your vision was going to resonate with a large number of potential customers. What was that 'because'? What was the special sauce you were bringing to the market that would guarantee your success and ability to compete?

If you're still using it, measure it! If you have found a better direction since, use the new one instead.

Like a fingerprint, the thing that makes your business different and special is also the thing (or combination of things!) that you need to keep the closest eye on. Some of these will be individual metrics, but some will call out interrelated data, such as our earlier example of a relationship between marketing budget and hiring schedule. Of course, that particular link may have no importance to you, but there will be some other delicate relationship between business activities that highlights a key element of your competitive advantage.

Once you have identified your KPIs, agree normal, alert and alarm or green / amber / red value ranges and make sure these can be represented graphically as a dial, pie chart or bar graph. More on this later when we look at Dashboards.

Finally, in order for KPIs to be as useful as possible, they need to be updated in real time. Let's examine that for a moment.

You'll recognise a long standing trope of office life, where an archetypal demanding and unreasonable boss dumps a load of files on some poor worker's desk and repeats the mantra "I need this report by tomorrow morning". We of course empathise with the long suffering employee whose evening has just been ruined by a manager who clearly can't see that people have lives outside work. The fact that it's such a well known theme means that it must happen often enough for it to be recognisable.

What possible reasons could a manager have for behaving in this way, other than the necessary level of disorganisation or petty spitefulness required for comedic purposes? Let's look at it from their point of view for a moment.

As a senior manager, what combination of circumstances could lead you to urgently need the kind of complex information it would take someone else a number of hours to assemble and probably also interpret? Does 'not having essential decision making information right at hand', plus 'an unexpected and high impact situation has arisen, needing a fast response' fit the bill?

Sounds pretty bad, right? Nobody wants to be put in a position where they have to make an important decision at short notice with incomplete (or even non existent) information. It's little wonder that our ostensibly wayward boss might seem a little stressed!

The point here, as you've probably already guessed, is to make sure that the information most likely to highlight something amiss is provided in an easy to digest form, directly from the source as live data. In other words, the whole concept of creating regular reports by hand is abandoned.

To close this section, a word on compliance. Specifically, should you include compliance data in your KPIs?

This varies hugely depending on the your business and the sector it operates in. Some industries are heavily regulated, others less so. All businesses have some regulatory requirements, but some have a large amount. Since the objective of KPIs is to identify the few most significant measurements that illustrate how your business is performing, it's up to you to decide whether compliance is key in this regard. Since compliance metrics are more about risk exposure than operational behaviour, you may decide to skew your few KPIs to other more performance oriented information.

SCOPE AND HORIZON

Let's look again at the decision hierarchy described earlier. We have already established that your business vision and mission are right at the top of the list, which has one more implication:

Your visionary level planning has infinite Scope and Horizon.

By Scope, I mean the proportion of the business affected, and by Horizon, the timescale over which the decision is expected to apply. In other words, the decisions and assumptions at the top of the hierarchy encompass all others, while at the same time having no limits to scope and horizon. This means the first decisions you make affect the entirety of the business, forever.

Why is this important? Because you need to remain aware that each subsidiary decision will have increasingly less scope and horizon, as it contributes to the decision above it.

To take a simple example, your 3 month business plan has a shorter horizon than your 1 year plan, which in turn has a shorter horizon than your 3 year plan and so on. Likewise, the scope of your marketing plan will have most impact on the marketing team, somewhat less in sales and less again in operations. That's not the same as saying no impact, just progressively less.

When thinking about forward looking decisions, you should be clear about their scope and horizon. This is because their supporting assumptions will also have scope and horizon, or in other words some limits on the degree to which they should be considered accurate and reliable. Why is this useful in management? Because it'll prevent you ending up with decision paralysis. If the decisions you need to make have a known scope and horizon, then their supporting assumptions can as well. While it's prudent to think widely about the assumptions that might impact your decision, you don't need to be held prisoner by assumptions that could reasonably be expected to fall outside the relevant scope and horizon.

For instance, businesses bound by formal contract will typically include a Force Majeure clause. You can look at this as a recognition that while they have been appropriately diligent with their service delivery, they explicitly recognise that events can occur that could not reasonably be anticipated and are making this clear to their customers or partners. In other words, they have set a scope for the assumptions around carrying out their business, and specifically excluded everything else from their liability.

To go back to my favourite snail safety business example. If I launch in the UK, an area not noted for its geological instability, it would be reasonable to assume that business won't be impacted by a volcano erupting under our head office. While I could try to incorporate some planning around torrents of lava scorching the carpet and turning the coffee to sulphuric steam, it's more sensible to exclude it from the list of things that are worth worrying about.

Let's go back to our original business plan, and think about its contents again in the context of all the new operational information we have at our fingertips.

We can now ask some useful questions, with a reasonable expectation of being able to answer them:

- To what extent were the original assumptions in our plan correct?
- To the extent they were not correct, what impact has that had on the plan?
- What changes do we need to make to the plan to hit our original goals?
- Are those changes realistic and practical, i.e. achievable?
- Are our original goals still realistic and practical, i.e. achievable?
- If not, what should our long term goals now be?
- What interim steps will help us get there?

You can see that the answers to these questions have varying scopes and horizons. You may be wondering why we're going into this degree of depth on this topic. This is why:

The biggest decisions have the furthest horizon and the widest scope, i.e. they affect the whole of the business over an extended period, that's what makes them big. However, this also means that the corresponding assumptions also have to have substantial scopes and horizons. They need to be widely valid for a long time!

Remember that the cost of being wrong before you launched was comparatively low. You made some sweeping statements and backed them up as best you could, but the costs involved in getting that far were limited. The launch period would have provided useful feedback on those assumptions, but of course you were trading by then, so the costs of error were significantly higher.

Now, after a meaningful period of business operations, there is a larger risk element associated with being wrong in your forecasts. You may well have staff, stock, equipment, premises, loans and so on and responsibilities to go with them. A decision making blunder here puts all you have achieved at risk as well as expected future rewards!

All of the above points to the need to make sure that the assumptions supporting your forward looking predictions have appropriate scope and horizon, and are tested in that context.

YOUR DATA IS YOUR BUSINESS

You can see by now that your data is pretty important stuff. It's hard to capture, but capture it you must if you want to understand how your business is performing today and predict how it will perform in the future. However I would go a lot further than that.

Your data IS your business.

Look at it this way. Although you would probably prefer not to, you could replace anything else in your business if you had to. People, premises, stock, equipment, even customers could in principle be replaced if they were lost to some situation or bad outcome.

The one thing - the ONLY thing you cannot replace if it's lost or stolen is your data.

Your data is everything there is to know about your business. Its operations, customers, suppliers, partners, staff, regulatory and financial position, trading history, credit rating and so on and so on. If your data is lost for any reason, you have no verifiable records to rebuild from, and verifiable is the critical attribute. Oh sure, you will remember a lot about much of it but the point is you can no longer show comprehensive and consistent records. In other words, whatever you remember is worthless. This is why ransomware attacks are so devastating and difficult to recover from.

What this all means is that protecting your data is not in any sense a luxury or something you can put off till next week. For all practical purposes the loss of your data equals the total loss of your business. How long are you willing to accept that risk?

You may well be thinking that data protection is a technology function, so it's something you can leave to your technology team. Not so. Data protection is a management function and lies within the realm of governance and risk management. Yes you can delegate the technical aspects to the IT team, but not all. For example;

- How much of your data should be backed up? All of it? Even operational data with limited shelf life? More comprehensive backups means more effective recovery but more storage costs and complexity.

- How often? More frequent backups also means more effective recovery but again more storage costs and complexity.

- What data protection policies do you have in place? For example, are your team allowed to store data on USB devices? Are they allowed to email files to personal email accounts? If so, how are you going to protect yourself against data theft?

- Do you have a data recovery plan? If so, who is authorised to initiate it? Under what conditions? Who needs to be informed and do they understand their role in the recovery process?

- Do you have a communications plan? Do you know how you are going to brief your team, your customers, your suppliers and partners while a business wide recovery process is under way? What about when normal operations have been restored?

This is all pretty heavy stuff, and a lot to take on board if you haven't thought about it from a management perspective before. However there is good news for the busy business leader. You don't need to reinvent the wheel, cyber certification is here to help. Regardless of where you operate and the size and complexity of your business, there will a cyber certification suitable for your needs. Alongside the technical stuff, certification addresses data protection policy and completing the certification process gives you a solid foundation for a data protection strategy specific to the needs of your business.

Any further exploration of cyber security and certification is outside the scope of this book, but I would urge you to talk with your technology partner and review your cyber protection provision.

One last point before we move on. While you can take out business cyber insurance, please keep in mind that insurance is by definition retrospective. It only takes effect after something bad has happened. While you may indeed be entitled to an insurance payment after a successful cyber attack, the more pertinent question is whether it's already too late by that point. I'll leave that one with you to ponder!

BUSINESS PROCESS

THE PRODUCTIVE HOUR

Having spent some time examining the value of business data to the management team, is that the end of the story? What benefits might accrue to the rest of your team from instant access to stored information? We're going to look at how access to information makes your team more effective, and by extension your business more profitable.

Ignoring the cost, would your business be able to do more today if it had more people? Now think about your long term growth targets. How many more people will that need?

For many businesses, the amount they can achieve, produce or deliver is a function of the number of people in their team. Although the relationship isn't necessarily linear, more people frequently equals more business, or at least more business often means you're going to need more people. And while many businesses look at people as an unavoidable cost, in truth, your people are your revenue generators.

Now, as we all know, finding the right people for your business is typically expensive, slow, and frustrating, so making the people you already have as effective as possible makes good, solid sense.

Making your people more effective is going to be tricky unless you have some means for understanding how effective they are today. Let's build a simple model to measure this so we can apply it right across the business.

Everyone in your team must contribute more than they earn, otherwise you wouldn't have a business. In other words, they have a net positive value. What we're going to do is compare the amount of value that a team member delivers into your business compared to what they cost. If you compare those two numbers, you get an idea of what that net value will be.

So on the basis that the costs associated with people are typically expressed as money, the value that they generate really should be able to be measured in money as well. Let's look at this in terms of cost versus income. Suppose you employ somebody at £30,000 a year, if their work generates £60,000 a year, then you can say their work is worth twice the salary. If we call this ratio a salary multiplier, then their salary multiplier would be two.

Now that's simple in principle, but in practice, measuring it can be a bit harder. Pick anybody in your business and ask yourself what the cash value is of the work they do for you. If you chose somebody in a sales team, it's fairly easy to measure, but if you pick somebody in an administrative role, it might be harder to come up with a figure. Then again, if you have somebody in an administrative role in a sales team, i.e. the sales administrator, if they stopped work and none of your sales people could work, then arguably, their salary multiplier is significantly higher than another administrator that wasn't in such a pivotal position.

So as you can see there's a degree of imagination and interpretation required here to work out to a reasonable approximation what somebody's salary multiplier should be. There is also a very simple way to do it, but it does hide some of the 'per head' or 'per department' nuance that might be helpful to understand as a manager.

In the most basic method, if you simply divide your turnover by the average salary across your team, then that gives you an overall salary multiplier for everybody in your business. On average, the salary multiplier per head will be whatever that number turns out to be.

Now, although this is useful for this particular part of the discussion, it's also not bad to have this or a similar KPI to have in your business. How much are you earning per head is a very good number to have available to you. It doesn't tell you a lot in detail, but it does tell you a lot about overall how well your business is performing, perhaps against other businesses in your industry or businesses of a similar size.

Now we tend to think about salaries in terms of so many pounds per year, but looking at salary multipliers on an annualised basis is not very helpful because to capture the information you have to look back i.e. wait until that year is complete to get your number. Still interesting but not super useful.

So let's break that down into something a bit more meaningful, specifically what that person's effectiveness would look like per hour. If you understand their effectiveness or productivity per hour, then anything that changes that figure per hour will be highly meaningful.

Let's look at costs first.

An example salary of say £30,000 a year, divided by 365 days by divided by 7 hours per day, comes out to a little less than £12 per hour. That's your salary cost at a surface level. However, that's not taking into account weekends, annual leave, public holidays, a few days for sickness, and so on. Adding workable values for those variables, our per hour salary cost is not £12, it's nearer £19 per hour.

The point here is this is just cost. This is what it costs to employ somebody and have them available to do work for you. So taking that number of £19 per hour, it's obviously in our interest to make that hour as effective as possible, i.e., to drive their salary multiplier up.

Now, what we're not going to do in this model is take into account individual performance or motivation. We'll assume that somebody you are paying is fully engaged in the task that they've been given. So let's work on the basis that somebody we're paying £19 per hour is working to capacity for that time.

If their calculated salary multiplier turns out to be two times, then per hour, this person will be earning you £38.

But anything you do to improve that multiplier will translate directly into more income every hour. And the reason for thinking about this on an hourly basis is that you can measure the effects of any changes you make quickly.

Consider the tasks that you employ your people to do, and I mean specifically about each person, not a general view of the tasks that the whole team undertake. Now think about the that tools person needs to be effective in their role.

I'm going to use the concept of tools a lot here. To be clear, tools does not necessarily mean physical tools. It's a generic term that means anything a person needs to do their job.

If somebody in your business needs digital information to

carry out their work, then you can look at that information and their computer as examples of the tools that they need to get the job done. So if you have someone in an admin role, for example, can they access all the information they need to work with? Can they see everything they need in a single glance? Or do they have to keep swapping backwards and forwards between different bits of information because they can't see it all at once? Do they have to keep stopping to wait for someone else to do something, or for their computer to finish what it's doing?

Making sure your people have the right information, the right tools, systems and processes will improve their salary multiplier. It will make them more effective.

The point here is that even though replacing, updating or implementing new working tools can feel expensive from a capital cost point of view, that cost will almost certainly be massively less than the productivity benefits it brings.

This is not obvious, so let's break it down a little.

If you consider a given productivity gain, i.e. salary multiplier improvement per hour, and look at the number of productive hours in a year, you'll see even small gains will add up to a very significant number in that period. Now take the cost of whatever tools or systems that person needs to do their job, and average it out over its useful lifespan. Looked at in the context of the productivity bonuses they bring, you'll see information handling tools tend to work out very cheap indeed. In other words, they're not a net cost, they are a net benefit!

Having looked at the benefits of productivity or efficiency improvements and captured the idea of a salary multiplier and seen how it applies to the work that your people do, it's also important to understand the concept of downtime. Downtime is simply a catch all term for the impact of losing those tools for some period.

We've already seen that an hour of somebody's time has pounds per hour value, as well as a pounds per hour cost. If for some reason, they're not able to work for one hour, you not only lose the hours worth of value that they would have brought you also retain the hours worth of cost that they automatically incur.

It's unusual to be able to send somebody away and stop paying them for one hour while their tools or environment or something else is fixed, so for practical purposes you're stuck with that cost.

So it's worth taking time out to think about mitigating downtime. How are you as a management team going to address the issues of downtime? It's important to note here that downtime is pretty much inevitable. Scenarios that you could not foresee will happen. Systems that you rely on will still fail. Negative impacts are inevitable and there will be downtime in the business.

Planning for downtime has two aspects to consider, prevention and recovery. Prevention requires actively lowering the risk of downtime for all the tools that you already know about, production environments already in your business and scenarios you can think of. For each of these, what steps might you take to avoid.

It's also worth giving some thought to what if the things that you haven't thought of yet, the things that have never bitten you yet.

What if this thing went wrong? What if that thing broke or got stolen?

Now you won't necessarily be able to come up with effective plans for what to do in each of those circumstances, but it is helpful to come up with a response mindset, a way of being able to say, "Well, we didn't think of this, but we've already thought about what we might do in a similar scenario, therefore we have some prior learning to get ourselves back up and running."

So what can you do to address issue of predictable downtime? Well, there are a number of ways forward here. Obviously, every business is different. The tools that you use are different, the impacts of downtime will be different, but making sure that for your team, the tools in use are fit for purpose, i.e. unlikely to fail through overuse or misuse. The wrong tool that got you out of trouble today might do it again tomorrow, but if you keep using it for three weeks then it will very likely fail.

I'm still using tools in the most general sense to represent whatever it is your people need to get their work done. Take preventative measures to make sure that whatever tools they use are maintained. That could be physical maintenance or whatever preventative measures or services are recommended by a manufacturer to prevent failure.

To take a nightmare example, if you have a building where everybody works, with fire alarms, burglar alarms, fire suppression systems and security of every description. Nothing you can imagine will prevent that building catching fire or being broken into etc.

What if the drains back up? What if there's a problem with

the sewers and the public health authorities say, "Right, that's it. You have to leave your building right now, we don't know when we'll be able to let you in again."

You might say that would never happen. Indeed it might not. But it conceivably could, and never is a long time. Imagining scenarios where some diligent forward planning would save you having to make some possibly shaky decisions in an emergency is a sensible precautionary measure.

Now, of course there are limits. It's easy to imagine preventative measures that wouldn't be cost effective when compared with the costs of downtime. To take my example of a building that suddenly became unavailable. It has all of your computers in it. It has all of your files or whatever you need in it, your tools, your workshops, everything.

You could in theory, have a whole spare building with computers and tools and everything else you need. Would that solve the problem? Yes absolutely. Would it be cost effective? Probably not.

So again, when thinking about what to do in the event of downtime situations, it's helpful to imagine all possible scenarios, compare them with all possible preventative measures, and make an conscious choice whether each one is cost effective.

Hopefully it's clear why this is a management function, not a technology one. Your technology team might be tasked with implementing any recovery planning you have in place, but a data driven management view of productivity should be combined with a corresponding business protection strategy.

BUSINESS COMMUNICATION

Have you ever wondered how email outgrew its usefulness as your business went from brilliant idea to the thriving enterprise it is today? As your team grew and the net complexity of business operations increased, managing email frequently becomes an unsupportable burden.

Why is this?

When you first launched, everybody knew everything. It was a small team, quite likely all working in the same space so that level of synchronisation was pretty much baked in. The big advantage here is that 100% shared knowledge means decision making becomes easy and therefore fairly quick. That's fine and a great advantage in the early days where little is known for sure and the ability to make rapid decisions is key to your success, but there is a hidden assumption here that's going to cause problems. Simply put, the assumption is that everyone knowing everything is both achievable and worth having forever.

What is our evidence for this?

- Reply All.
- Cc world + dog.
- Forwarding FYI

...and so on. These are simply 'best effort' attempts to ensure that everyone knows everything, at least in the context of a given message.

Why does this matter?

Let's take a team of 5 people. If everyone is able to directly message everyone else, and every message is regarded as important to everyone, then a single sent message will be received 4 times. In other words, the sender just created 4 tasks for other people from a single personal task. If everyone sends a message, there are now 20 tasks for the team to carry out. The task in each case is to assess the message and make a judgement on whether an action is required, and this is just for one message each. Also keep in mind the effort disparity between sending and receiving an email. It takes almost no work to make a reply a Reply All, cc or an FYI, but a lot more work collectively to receive that email and decide what to do with it.

No wonder email workloads spiral wildly out of control!

Now think about your business at 10x its current size. Let's assume that you now employ 50 people and everyone is emailing everyone else. Does this sound like a scalable solution? Well clearly it must be because there are very large organisations that still rely on email, but ask anyone who works in a corporate environment about the amount of time they spend on email and watch their face contort in pain. I hope we can safely agree that something better than email is needed.

But hang on a moment, this is not about email, it's about communication. If we can consciously abandon the idea of everybody needing to know everything, we're able concentrate on making sure everyone knows what they need to know.

What do they need to know? Well, enough to get their job done.

We'll come back to what that means shortly, but for now we're going to look at business communication itself and ask some more questions about what needs communicating and why.

One of the fundamental principles of a business is to be able to do whatever you do over and over again in order to make the most money for the least effort. To take an extreme example, if I ran a successful insurance broker and tried to break into the pet accessories industry, I'd likely fail because nothing in my existing business could help me compete, nor would my credibility in insurance make anyone inclined to buy pet supplies from me. So when considering day to day operations, efficient repetition is a good objective.

Then again, with the best will in the world and much as you'd like to, you can't guarantee repeatability. Things will go wrong, whether under your control or not, and new things will happen that you hadn't anticipated. It's worth taking a moment to expand on that second point.

When you start your new venture, you're working in a comparatively low complexity environment. You're only doing a few things, and not that many of them. Obviously you're planning to do more but for now, one cycle of whatever you do looks pretty much like the last one and the next one. Now that's fine and as it should be, but there's a hidden element that needs to be recognised. The assumption is that a known task is 100% identical every time it is executed. This is, regrettably, not true.

You see, although we think about work tasks individually in order to make them manageable, they can't actually exist in complete isolation. There will always be inputs and outputs, changing conditions and situations. Not least, people can't act with guaranteed repeatability. If Janine's 90 year old grandmother won a gymnastics competition last night or Brian had to deal with his son's hamster unexpectedly mauling the family Rottweiler, do you think either of them will perform precisely the same today as they did yesterday?

So regardless of cause, slight variations in how a task is carried out should be expected. For a simple task, it might be 1 in every 10,000 iterations, i.e. for whatever reason, 1 time in 10,000 the result of a given task is not what was expected. For a more complex operation with many steps or interactions, it might be 1 in 20. The point here is it's effectively impossible to predict in advance how perfectly repeatable a given task will be. All you can do is run it many times and measure what you discovered.

So if we call tasks that behave completely as expected 'workflow', let's call those that exhibit rare or unexpected behaviour 'edge cases'.

Now let's examine what happens when things actually go wrong. What do I mean by 'wrong'? This is the catch all category for events requiring supervisory or management intervention. For example a customer complaint (or several!) or a stoppage in production operations. By definition, these are not predictable. If they are then it's within the role of management to take appropriate steps to prevent further occurrences. Since these examples all need escalation to a more senior decision maker, we'll just call them 'escalations'.

We've categorised the vast majority of day to day business operations, so what about those that haven't happened yet? What about forward looking or planning activity? After all, we're all about growing the business so the prospect of tomorrow not looking like today is kind of built in. We need to recognise a whole branch of business activity around management and decision making.

Finally, what about the informal chats and discussions that make the workplace a fun environment to be in? These are frequently cited as a reason to return to office based or similar working after working from home became so widespread in recent years. Whether these chats take place in person over the proverbial water cooler (for the curious, The Proverbial Watercoolers is my new band name) or on video chat, happen they will. If people are going to be social in discussion, then they are going to be social when messaging. That's pretty much guaranteed.

So what have we ended up with here? A simplified model for internal business communications. Please note - I have excluded external communications on purpose for now. As follows:

- Workflow
- Edgecases & escalations
- Management tasks
- Water cooler

Having got this far, what communications tools do we have available for use?

Your mileage may vary, but as a representative sample:

- Face to face
- Phone
- Paper memo / noticeboard / markerboard
- Email
- External messaging system (SMS or WhatsApp for example)
- Internal messaging system (MS Teams or similar)
- Workflow management software

You may have all of these in your organisation or just some.

As your business grows in size and complexity, we have shown you will inevitably have to cope with exponentially more internal communications, relating to the four different categories above. Using this communications model, and recognising that communications should have meaning and value and be sent with intent, it's important to take the opportunity to set some rules or policies around who should send what to who, when and why.

This is where we return to my earlier point about what people actually need to know. In the context of all the options above, you can now see why abandoning 'everybody knowing everything' is not just a logical step but actually a crucial aspect of business growth. If we embrace this, it sets us free to look again at internal communications in the specific context of who needs to know what.

By way of contrast, while having timely, accurate information is essential, receiving and having to process information you don't really need is both a productivity drain as well as a gigantic pain in the… well it's just an unnecessary distraction and we can leave it there.

What other policies might be useful?

Well, just because functions like cc and Reply All are available, doesn't mean they should be used. Or at least, used on an ad hoc basis. Remember, people like to be helpful, and sharing information widely feels like being helpful. It's only when the operational impacts of doing this on an uncontrolled basis are taken into account that the associated problems become clear.

So how are we going to manage this? Let's go back to our old friend, the customer journey.

Using the customer journey as a framework, we can make some sensible observations about what Workflow, Edge Cases and Escalations ought to look like. For each step from Marketing to Billing / Post Sale it should be easy to understand who is doing what, and by extension what information they need to carry out that task to a high standard. The next step is to deduce which communications tool is most appropriate for that kind of messaging. We will look at this again when we investigate process management tools.

Having worked through the customer journey model, you can take all your back office functions and run the exercise again.

Next, a policy set is also helpful for communication relating to management and planning. On the basis that this kind of activity is important yet not repetitive, careful thought is required to avoid a lot of well intentioned but unstructured messaging. However, the principle of 'what you need to get the job done' still applies.

Finally, what are you going to do about social / team building / 'water cooler' chat? Again, you have two decisions to make here. The first is which communications method is most appropriate, and the second is the policy set around it. What kind of chat meets your teams' natural desire to be sociable but also works within your business policies and company values? For example, if a team wide 'good morning' is fine, and good morning with a smiley face emoji is also OK, is every emoji acceptable? Do bear in mind you may be legally liable for content shared on an internal system. Alternatively, if these kinds of messages are shared on an external system, you have no control over what gets uploaded or indeed who gets to see it.

TELEPHONY

We've spent some time examining written communications and the different types in common use. These all sit in a category we call asynchronous, which simply means that information can be sent and received at different times. While being able to send a message and not having to worry whether the recipient is available to receive it immediately is a huge boon in a busy business, as we have already seen it can cause unintended bottlenecks.

So if that's asynchronous communication, what does synchronous look like?

How about picking up the phone?

The definition of synchronous communication is that the sender and receiver are involved at the same time. If one or the other of you isn't available to talk, then communication just doesn't happen. To be clear, leaving voicemail falls back into the asynchronous category since by definition the sending and receiving happen at different times.

In a world seemingly completely dependent on messaging in its many and varied forms, do we even need to speak to each other any more? I'm kidding of course. It's hard to imagine a business running without any kind of voice services, so let's look at those next.

Once again, I'm not going to go too far into the technology of modern business telephony. While it's certainly interesting to the technically minded, our focus as always is how such systems become useful to business. Suffice to say, the generic term for digital telephony is VoIP or Voice Over IP. IP is the underpinning technology that the whole internet runs on, hence voice services using this technology pick up that description.

So what does a business leader need to be aware of when thinking about telephony services?

The first thing to take into account is understanding how your voice services reach you. For all practical purposes, gone are the days when a telephony provider would install a separate box on your wall for you to connect your desk handset to. Modern phone systems are digital from one end to the other which means they are delivered via your internet connection. It's worth keeping this in mind when thinking about the quality and resilience of your internet service. An outage will probably take your phones down as well as your email and any other centralised way of keeping in touch!

So what are the principal differences between traditional analogue telephony and its modern digital replacement?

- Policy based call handling
- Management reporting
- Portability and device freedom
- Business software integration
- Call recording

I'll explain policy based call handling by using the example of a startup business.

You'll probably remember right back in the beginning of your business, when there was just a single public facing phone number for the entire enterprise and your team used their mobile phones to stay in touch as often as not. Once again, the launch of a new business is a time when costs need to be kept to a minimum and the best tools to use are the ones people are already comfortable with. So this start scenario makes perfect sense.

Let's assume your launch is a great success, and your single phone is constantly busy with new customer enquiries. It would be really handy to have two handsets that both rang when a new call came in. Simple in principle, right? But what you're looking at here is your first example of policy based call handling. Your new policy is; both handsets respond to the same inbound number and both will ring when that number is called. Let's wind the clock forward 12 months and assume your success has continued. You now have 8 people available to answer customer calls, however you might not want every phone to ring every time. For instance, if one of your team wants to make an outbound call but can't because their phone is constantly ringing with inbound queries. In this situation, it would be good to be able to set someone's phone status as 'busy' to allow them to concentrate on outbound calls. Needless to say, that's another call handling policy.

Now let's look at the remaining people on the team. Is their job exclusively or even mainly focused on answering the phone? If some of them have other, more urgent work to do and call answering is something you want them to do only if everyone else is busy, then you might want to create a policy that says phones 1 - 5 ring immediately but phones 6 - 8 only ring if 1 - 5 are busy.

What we're doing here is building up a set of call handling policies that are closely tailored to the needs of your business and can be updated quickly and easily as your requirements change. While being able to make these changes is a good thing, it's the quickly and easily part that makes all the difference. That's where operational flexibility lives!

You can imagine that a policy set could easily become quite complicated, and while that may sound like a bad thing, it actually reflects some truly great outcomes. If your business is so successful that you need an elegant policy set to ensure the most effective use of your customer facing team to deliver a great customer experience, then you're clearly winning!

OK, so you have a busy call handling team, benefiting from a policy based rule set. You might well want to know more about how effective those rules really are, and whether they could be tweaked for better performance. Equally, you might want to know about the individual call handling performance of everyone on that team, with annual reviews and similar in mind. As with modern software, up to date VoIP systems have extensive reporting capabilities. These are usually presented in two forms, wallboards and reports. Wallboards are large display screens with up the minute call handling stats and are most frequently seen in call centres where instantaneous stats are very important. While your own business may not need physical wallboards, the call handling logic they're built on can generate useful statistical call performance metrics to aid forecasting and capacity planning.

So if that's how we describe the set of rules that manage our calls, how do we physically make them? We've had handsets on our desks for years, what do today's options look like? This is where the good news really kicks in. Simply put, if phone calls are managed in software, they can be made and received in software as well. What this means is that anything that can run an app can in theory be used as a business phone as well. So your business phone can live as a program on your PC and on your mobile device as well as on a desk handset with absolutely no difference in behaviour or performance.

It's worth taking another look at your startup business to understand an important implication here. Remember when you had limited phone capacity and everyone used their mobiles as often as not? While that's an economical way to get started, it does create its own complications which can quickly become major headaches.

If one of your team makes an external call from their mobile, will the recipient associate that number with your business? After all, your public phone number may well be a highly visible part of your brand, don't you want it to become recognised so recipients always know who they're talking to when they answer a call? In addition, if customers, suppliers or partners start relying on individual mobile numbers to reach your company, how will you maintain records of who called when and what was said? More on this in a moment but you can see that having multiple phone numbers associated with your business may not be a good thing.

To understand how entrenched this issue is, just look through the stack of business cards you have been given over time. How many of them list a separate mobile number for that person? It's quite a few if not most, right? So if you wanted to call someone, which number should you use? Based on their business card you have no idea whether they prefer to be called on their mobile or their desk phone, or whether their mobile is for emergencies only and so on. While trying to be helpful, they are unintentionally making your life harder and purely as a result of having poorly managed business telephony.

So how are you going to avoid this mess yourself? By mandating that all business calls should be made through the core telephony system, and making sure that the app for that system is available for every device that could reasonably be needed for making calls. While this might seem a tad heavy handed at first sight, it actually makes people's lives easier.

Firstly, while they may choose to continue using their own mobile device for business calls, the fact that the call is being made from an app means their mobile number is no longer disclosed when doing so. If this is also a personal mobile number that's actually a big deal. Next, using an app to make calls uses internet data rather than call minutes. While this is less of an issue than it used to be, generous data allowances with mobile packages mean that calls don't use up whatever monthly minutes are included with their phone service. If you are paying or reimbursing their mobile phone bill then of course this may not be a problem. However, if not...!

Now everyone on your team can present a business card with a single number on it, and anyone trying to call them will automatically know that they are guaranteed the best chance of reaching that person regardless of where they are. Doesn't that look a lot more professional?

Now if we're looking at the phone just being a piece of software, independent of the device used to physically answer the call, what else can we do to make life easier? And by easier of course I mean more efficient. Well how about having your phone software work directly with your business software? This is not a particularly new trick, but it's not as widely adopted as you might think considering its advantages.

A typical scenario might be an incoming call automatically triggering a search in your customer management system, such that a recognised number automatically calls up that customer's record before you answer the call, complete with details of their last few conversations with you. Does that sound like a great starting point for a good customer experience? Alternatively, in an outbound calling situation, how about being able to call someone with a single click directly from the piece of software you're using? Again, a call is taking place right in the centre of all the information needed to make that call a success.

How many times have you heard a friend or colleague mention a frustrating call experience with a company? By frustrating I don't just mean taking a long time to get to speak to someone (although that certainly doesn't help!), but more specifically trying to explain what they needed to an agent who didn't have the information they needed to be able to assist. When this already disastrous call subsequently gets transferred to someone else, only for the whole discussion to start again from scratch, you can't blame people for getting seriously irate.

If your business is going to avoid becoming another customer complaint magnet, you need to make sure that customer interactions are as efficient as possible since efficiency in these examples equals a good caller experience.

While we're talking about customer experience, we should include call recording. One of the facilities that digital telephony makes easy is making recordings of inbound and outbound calls. After all, we're all used to enjoying music streaming services at home, which simply store audio as files and play them back on demand. Recording and playing back phone calls uses a similar principle.

Now call recording is most often regarded at best as a defensive tool, allowing you to evidence who said what to who and when, and thus protect yourself against unfounded customer accusations or complaints, and at worst as a necessary evil as part of your industrial compliance requirements. One of the reasons this has been true is that while making recordings is comparatively easy, indexing their content without playing them back and making notes has been more or less impossible until very recently. What this means is that the effort involved in actually using existing recordings is high enough that it's only carried out when something has already gone wrong i.e. a customer has complained. The important point here is that the role of call recording in business has been shaped by its operational limitations not by its potential usefulness.

Now imagine if every call was not just recorded but indexed automatically. This means having a full transcript available without needing to listen to the recording first. Wouldn't it be wonderful to be able to search large volumes of calls for positive keywords or phrases like 'you were really helpful' or 'you've been great' and so on? Let's take that up a notch. Suppose there were AI based applications that could scan your call recordings for you and summarise tone and make a sensible guess at satisfaction.

As you'll have guessed, this isn't a wild supposition on my part. These applications exist today, and offer you the option to make call recording an active, forward looking part of your customer service objectives. If you are in a position to be able to both coach and reward your team on an evidenced basis, won't they go even further to delight your customers? I'll leave that one with you to contemplate.

PROCESS AUTOMATION

So on the basis that our people have all the information they need to do their job (and no more!), what does their job actually look like? Are they doing the same task over and over again or are no two days alike? How much discretion do they have in how their work carried out? Are they allowed, expected or even required to handle their own edge cases and escalations?

It's time to look at business processes, or how you do what you do on a repeatable basis.

As previously mentioned, all other things being equal one of the key differences between a successful business and a struggling business is its ability to execute repeatably, reliably and efficiently. However, very few businesses start out efficient and reliable. There is inevitably a period of experimentation and adjustment while the best ways of doing things becomes apparent. During this early stage your people have to both execute and adapt which means, among other things, that their workload is not highly repetitive. However, over time this position will change as learning is gained and best practice is established. In other words, from a highly fluid beginning, your people will be tasked with ever increasing degrees of routine work.

This transition may happen over quite a long period which means it's easy to miss. However, since it's pretty much inevitable, it's worth thinking about how to take best advantage and make it work for you.

Before we move on, let's look again at people and their strengths and weaknesses. You'll remember the slightly colourful example of Brian's hamster from earlier (at least I hope you do, I can't get that image out of my mind!). The point is that Brian, an otherwise diligent and detail focused member of the team, may not have brought his A game this morning when it comes to concentrating on his work. At least, not if his work requires him to carry out the same task over and over again.

Of course I'm being unfair on Brian, but the point I'm making is this. Even your best, most reliable people can have off days and their ability to carry out their work without error is not guaranteed.

There is a particular category of repetitive tasks that people are uniquely bad at, and I need to highlight it here. That category is data processing. What counts as data processing? Basically it's reading, entering or translating raw data. There are two main issues here. To begin with, people are both very slow and error prone when typing, at least when compared with a computer. It's even worse when it comes to reading. Ohs and zeros look the same on a page, as do ones and ells. Commas and full stops are easily mistaken, and the list goes on. In a situation where someone has to read the contents of a computer screen, carry out some kind of translation or processing on that information in a spreadsheet and then type the results into another system (this happens more often than you'd think) then you're looking at a worst of all worlds scenario. It's slow, error prone, unreliable and possibly worst of all, you can't report on it - manually processed data becomes less reliable for decision making purposes.

Bottom line, try as hard as you can to avoid manual data processing taking place in your business.

So if people are not ideally suited to highly repetitive tasks, how are we going to get them done? Well unsurprisingly, we need to find some way to automate them. Where people can get tired, or ill or distracted, machines don't. Now that's all very well I hear you say, but what if there are complexity or cost barriers to automating what we do? Brian's just going to have to suck it up and knuckle down at the same time.

Now before we go off the deep end into some automation wonderland, let's have a reality check.

Is it possible to automate every task in our workflow? No? Does that mean we can't benefit from process automation? Even if we can automate, will it be worth it? I.e. what's the payback period on the investment?

To examine these questions, it's time to go back to workflow, edge cases and escalations and think about them in the context of how they might be automated. Let's begin with a mark in the sand. Let's assume for the purposes of discussion that 80% of the tasks on the customer journey are repeatable enough that they could be automated, and the remaining 20% is edge cases and escalations. Please note - I'm not suggesting that these are desirable or even acceptable proportions, they just give us some easy numbers to work with.

So if you manage to automate the most routine 80% of your workflow, that puts you in an interesting position. Firstly it means that those tasks will almost certainly be done faster and with a lower error rate than Brian can do them. Secondly, any task automation system should be able to generate reports on how those tasks were carried out, i.e. with analysis, trend data and so on. Hey look, free decision making fuel!

It also frees Brian up to carry out the kind of work that people are generally more suited to. Specifically, work that requires imagination, context, judgement and interpretation. In other words, edge cases and escalations.

There is something else to point out here, and it's a biggie.

Everything we're talking about is in the context of a growing business. This has a couple of implications. Firstly, rare events that fall into the edge cases category today because they only happen once every 3 months, will happen increasingly more often as your business grows, to the extent that they will at some point fall into the 80% of routine tasks and are therefore worth the effort of automating..

What just happened here?

Your business grew by enough that a rare event is now so common it can be automated - WITHOUT needing more people.

So now we understand the relationship between business growth, edge cases and process automation, we should consider how best to handle escalations.

To begin with, while you probably wouldn't want to go around creating them on purpose, the often missed benefit from escalations (remember these are examples of things going genuinely wrong) is they are an opportunity to improve your process quality.

Again, this is where Brian's skill and context comes to bear. He has lots of experience in how things are supposed to work, so when something goes off the rails, he's ideally placed understand the root cause of what went wrong which consequently means he can improve and update the process.

This will tend to drive escalations down which in turn drives product or service quality up.

Have you ever had a bad experience with a company, or heard from a friend who has, only for your complaint to be handled so well that your opinion of that company actually goes up not down? Suppose you ring up to complain, and you get to speak to someone immediately. Not just anybody, but someone who can find out what has gone wrong quickly, understand what's needed to put it right and has the authority to do so.

Since you're a reasonable person, and you understand that sometimes things just go wrong, what you want is some remedial outcome that adequately addresses the degree to which the failure has affected you. If you end up getting that, or preferably somewhat more, then that's a good outcome.

In order for this to happen, you need someone with the skills, experience and authority of Brian. On the basis that part of his role is deciding what workflow activities are worth automating and how best to do it, his expertise can turn a poor customer experience into a good one. However, the crucial point here is that the root cause is both understood in the context of normal workflow, and that workflow is amended to incorporate the set of conditions that led to the failure in the first place.

It's worth noting at this point that I haven't distinguished between physical processes, i.e. handling materials and digital i.e. information processing. This is entirely on purpose as the principles are the same in each case even if the financial dynamics around the solutions may not be. After all a piece of production line machinery might cost a lot more than a new piece of software but if the long term benefit is clear then the capital cost is not the key driver.

In the context of everything we have covered so far, it's time to take a fresh look at business software.

SOFTWARE, HARDWARE AND SERVICES

SOFTWARE TYPES

If you walk into any office building, you won't be in the least surprised to see the majority of people using Microsoft Office or Google Docs to carry out their work. Spreadsheets, emails and presentations, we're all so used to them that we never stop to ask why. So let's do that now.

Why? Why are these specific apps used so widely?

Hey, we're on a roll here. Let's ask a few more pertinent questions.

Are these software titles the best option for the jobs they're being used for? Who said so?

Would Rembrandt have used a four inch brush to paint The Night Watch just because it came in handy for painting his garage? Would Michelangelo have carved his sculpture of David with the same chisel his brother Barry recommended for cutting bricks?

Probably not, although the resulting mental images are worth a moment's contemplation...

If it's easy to accept that there are correct and incorrect tools for physical jobs, it's not much of a leap to see that the same might be true of business software. Before we get into the difference between types of software and how they become useful, it's worth taking a moment to review how we got to where we are. Why are certain programs almost universal in an office setting?

There are two reasons for this, we'll start with history.

In the early days of computers in a business setting, very few software packages were even remotely applicable for business purposes, so those that were tended to be used for everything. Microsoft Word was more or less the only program that could write everything from a memo to a management report, so it became the default tool for all kinds of written document. Likewise with spreadsheets. The sheer utility of cell relationships made them massively useful for many numerical tasks.

However it's important to remember that these apps became universal because there were no workable alternatives, or at least no alternatives that could compete with Microsoft for market share.

The second reason derives from the first, which is that these common apps are effectively supplied with every business computer at an affordable price. This means that whether you start a new job or a new business, the computer you start with will almost certainly come with a set of software tools you are probably already quite familiar with. On that basis, this software represents a low cost, low risk way to get started.

However, in the same way you probably wouldn't expect to win a Formula One race in the first car you ever bought, the software you start out with can only get you so far and no further. So what software should you opt for? Do you really need to abandon all the apps you already understand?

Choosing business software is risky as well as difficult.

The purchase price is typically only a fraction of the overall cost of ownership. Consider training, installation, possible hosting or server requirements and that's not even taking into account the commercial value of the work you'll be using that software for.

To help make these choices significantly easier, I am going to create some categories for software and then fit typical examples into them. Once you see how they fit, you will more easily be able to categorise new offers and options and have a better chance of interpreting how well they could suit your business.

The categories are:

- General purpose
- Task aware
- Business aware
- Bespoke software

The first category is General Purpose software.

GENERAL PURPOSE

The defining characteristic of general purpose software is that each program can be used 'out of the box' for a reasonably wide variety of tasks. Take a word processor for example. With a modern word processing program, you could just as easily write a book or a newsletter or a restaurant menu.

This sounds great in principle, inasmuch as you only need one piece of software for lots of jobs. It's a veritable bargain, right? Well actually, no.

Let's begin with making documents useful.

When you create a document with a word processor, the document only 'knows' what it contains, not what it's for or why it has been created. In other words in order to understand what the document is for, you might need to ask the person that created it, or open it and read it.

You might be able to see the beginning of the problem. When using a document for business purposes, the information it contains is always about something. It has no meaning on its own. To put it another way, if I communicated the number 17 to you, it would be meaningless without context, i.e. what it related to. If you asked me how many sales I had made in the last hour, 17 might be a good number. If on the other hand you asked me how many customer complaints I had received in the last 10 minutes, 17 might be a very bad number indeed.

To go back to our newly typed document, to make it useful in a business context you would need to do one of three things. Either a) have some documented process that clearly states what any given document is for, b) ask the sender or tell the recipient what it relates to, or c) add some additional content within the document with the required context. In a production environment where efficiency is a desirable attribute, option a) is workable but options b) and c) are absolutely not. More on sharing information later.

To prove the above points and introduce a few more of great significance, we're going to address the big bad wolf of business software.

Spreadsheets.

Spreadsheets are the premium example of why general purpose software is ideal for a new or early stage business, and horrifically bad for an established one. On the evidence of widespread spreadsheet use in industry, this may be a controversial position to take. I need to go into some detail here to prove my point. Bear with me, it'll be worth it.

A spreadsheet is useful in principle because cells can contain any value, and the values they contain are related or tied together with simple logical statements. Based on your cell logic, a spreadsheet can be used to illustrate any set of relationships between cell data. While that is absolutely true, there are real world implications that undermine its usefulness.

Let's take the example of a spreadsheet Janine created to manage some simple but repeating task or other. In this scenario, the business she worked for had only recently launched, and repeatable processes were not well established. Being a diligent person, she noticed that this task happened on a repeating basis and had inputs and variables that could easily be typed in as numbers. Quite naturally, she created a quick spreadsheet to track inputs and outputs, and in just a few minutes she had a simple tool to help her manage that part of her work.

So far so good. Not only can she use this tool to manage her work, since there's only a limited amount of information she can also see its current status in a single glance.

This is where things start to go wrong.

Janine's manager Brian spots her working with this splendid new tool, and asks her to expand it to cover other departments as well. After all, if it can capture and manage the relationships between a limited set of data values, then it can do the same thing for a larger set, right?

Well yes, but it's not as simple as that. You see, when Janine first created her spreadsheet, even if she typed the input data without error its usefulness was only as good as the cell logic, and the cell logic was only as good as her understanding of the task at hand combined with her understanding of the software. If her understanding of either or both isn't perfect, then the cell relationships won't be perfect either.

This matters for two reasons. Firstly, as soon as a task or process is captured as a set of numbers, then those numbers tend to be relied on as the truth even though they are just a representation of the truth. So input or typing errors may not be spotted quickly. Secondly, the more cells you have in your sheet, the greater the number of possible relationships between them. That number grows exponentially not linearly. (For the morbidly curious, the number can be expressed as a formula: $x = n(n - 1) / 2$ where x is the number of possible relationships and n is the number of cells) Why is this important? Because it's a hint that complexity can quickly spiral out of control if you're not careful.

To illustrate. If there's a logical relationship between cell A1 and cell B1, then the contents of B1 are directly affected by the contents of A1. That's intuitively obvious because it's a simple relationship. You can go on to create a new relationship between B1 and C1, and as before you can say that C1 is also affected by A1. However, the value of C1 is now the result of two entirely independent cell relationships. Still not too bad I hear you say?

If its not hard to imagine cell A1 having increasingly indirect relationships with cells B1, B2, B3 and B4, what if B4 has further relationships with cells F17, N9, P23 and W212 and so on? The issue here is that while numerical values are clearly visible, the relationship logic is not. So a high degree of trust has to be placed in the original spreadsheet design.

Keep in mind that these relationships are actually representations of business processes and you start to see why the complexity of a large spreadsheet can become unmanageable for one person.

There is another reason why Janine might not fully understand the task at hand, and we've seen it before. Edge cases. Even if you're running what looks like a simple task, if you run it enough times you may find that it wasn't quite as simple as you thought. If your task does something weird once every 10,000 iterations and you've only run it 9000 times, you'll believe that you understand the behaviour of that task perfectly when in fact you don't.

If this is starting to sound bad, trust me it gets a lot worse.

So poor Janine now owns a spreadsheet that contains a lot more data than she originally set out to manage, which she can't necessarily verify the accuracy or quality of since it's outside her role. She may also have to create a larger set of cell logic rules, with correspondingly higher complexity. She also can't be sure her cell logic is correct because the task has only been run a few times. When I say she can't be sure, I really mean she can't be.

To the observer using a model to run a task there is no difference between that model being 100% perfect, and that model having an error that pops up less often than the number of times it has been run. In other words, she can't tell whether her logic is perfect or whether there's an error in it she just hasn't seen yet.

Is this sounding grim yet? Sit tight, there's more...

Let's think about her spreadsheet having two uses rather than one. It was originally created to help her manage a task she needed to carry out, and since it was a simple tool for a simple task, understanding the current status of the work at hand was as simple as looking at all the numbers in use and intuitively interpreting them for short term purposes i.e. minute to minute decision making. But we've seen that ability to interpret what's going on before. It's management reporting.

Brian has already seen that Janine has a useful tool for managing a task, and that it can be expanded to incorporate a larger set of data. Since his own work is focused around decision making, he is keen to use her data to help him. After all, these are numbers and numbers can always be trusted! However, looking at the newly expanded set of numbers, it's no longer possible to see at a glance what's going on. There's just too much information to interpret.

What Brian needs is a summary of these numbers to help him make decisions. A report.

As we know, spreadsheets are able to create graphs to represent sets of cell values, so all Janine needs to do is choose the cells Brian is interested in, and pick a suitable graph for them. Simple really!

Er, no. No its not. While using a graph to represent sets of cell values sounds easy, there's another whole set of logic required to achieve this. Which cells are the relevant ones?

When creating the graph, what relationships between cells should be chosen? The reason this becomes very difficult is that the report is not being created for Janine's own benefit, it's for Brian. In order for this report to be useful, Brian needs to understand his own reporting requirements and be able to describe them in sufficient detail that Janine doesn't have to do any interpretation when building the report.

What we end up with here is a cascading set of assumptions as follows:

Janine assumes she has typed in her own data without error. She also assumes that additional data she has to work with is also error free. She assumes that the logical relationships between spreadsheet cells is perfect and that the task itself repeats without variance however many times it's run. Brian assumes that he understands his own work requirements perfectly and that he has been able to translate them as a set of report requirements to Janine completely. Janine assumes that her report fully captures Brian's needs and he is happy with the output.

That's quite a stack of assumptions, any of which could be slightly or even grossly wrong, and on the basis this spreadsheet is going to be used a) to manage work that has a real world dollar value, and b) to help make predictions and forecasts that will likely have a much higher dollar value, the commercial risk around using it is significant!

Now let's extend the timescale out a bit and see how much worse this situation can really get. Let's roll the clock forward two years and see what's happening.

Since this spreadsheet was so useful in the beginning, it

has remained as a core part of the businesses' workflow management and reporting function to this day.

That's worth examining in itself. How much do you think a growing business will change in the course of two years? Quite a bit would seem a reasonable answer. So what we have now is a single spreadsheet carrying out a critical role in a business that no longer looks like the one it was created for. What are the chances that Janine or anyone else will go back and re-examine the original cell logic that the spreadsheet was based around, in the light of new working methods or trading conditions? What about the reporting requirements? If the core cell logic is changed for any reason, report values may well change even though the underlying data has not.

This is clearly a bit of a mess from a business and risk management point of view, and underlines why spreadsheets are not fit for purpose as a workflow management tool.

Before we leave this topic, I'd like to finish with a grand finale. In case you're thinking 'well yes it's mess but at least it works', Janine just handed her notice in.

If any of the inherent problems seemed bad before, they just got a lot worse.

You see it's quite likely that Janine is the only person in the business who ever knew how this monster spreadsheet of doom actually works. Although it's possible for someone else to 'take one apart' by looking at the cell relationships, you won't necessarily know why those relationships were chosen instead of any others. After all, this spreadsheet was originally created to help one person carry out one part of her own job. So long as it met that requirement, she didn't have to justify to anyone why it was built the way it was built. So there probably won't be any supporting documentation to refer back to.

How's your week going at this point?

Let's move on. We're going to look at data files in some detail to understand their limitations and operational impacts. We need to go into some depth here, and get a little closer to the world of IT but trust me, this is crucial insight for non technical business leaders.

General purpose software has one other attribute that adds to its overall lack of suitability for workflow tasks. What it creates are files. A spreadsheet is a file. A word processor document is a file and you'll find examples of this wherever you look. Now that may feel like such an obvious statement that you'll be thinking "yes, so what?".

Well, without even having to think about computers, data files create a whole set of problems on their own. We can consider them in two sets, problems with personal files and bigger much gnarlier ones that apply to shared files.

For personal files:

How are data changes and updates saved? Do you save your file every time a change is made? If so, does that save happen automatically or do you have to do it manually? If it's automatic, is the data complete and correct at the moment it is saved? To put this another way, if your file is saved automatically, the save process will over write earlier data. Is that necessarily what you wanted every time?

If saving is a manual task, can you guarantee you'll remember to do it every time and in the right place?

These points all contribute to one major issue. If you just save a file at specific times or workflow milestones, you lose your granular audit trail of what changes were made and when. This isn't the same as having multiple levels of 'undo'. If your operational model is to just overwrite a file when its contents change, your chances of successfully 'stepping back through time' to earlier saves to check that you're working with the correct version is at risk at best, and completely lost at worst.

You're probably thinking that there's an easy fix here. Every time you save the file with new data, just create a new version. Bingo! Now your audit trail is maintained! You can step back through earlier versions and compare data changes. Well yes, but then again, no. To begin with, comparing different files to find changes, although it's doable, is not necessarily quick or easy. You'll remember the points we established earlier looking at the productive hour. If you're error checking, you're no longer producing!

But there's a bigger issue to deal with. If you are creating multiple versions, how robust is your version naming convention?

My version what now?

If you are going to maintain your data audit trail by using multiple versions of your files, you're going to need some method of making sure that you know which file you are working with at any given time. You can either achieve this by giving the file a meaningful name, or give the place it is stored (i.e. a folder) a meaningful name. Again, that's fine, but what constitutes meaningful?

In order for you to be sure you're working on the right file, you need to have a way of naming all your files such that the right one is always easy to find. Sounds simple, at least until you consider how that's achieved.

You'll need to decide:

How the name of the file (I'll consider folder naming and file naming as the same thing here) describes both its purpose and contents, and makes clear which version it is. When describing its purpose and contents, you need to take into account that both of these may change over time as the file becomes more useful. So a file called 'customer shipping' or 'field service' might be a suitable description for a six month old business with three people, but by the time that company hits six years and thirty three people the scope of the data in that file may be huge and the original name may not reflect its purpose or contents any more.

When describing its version, you need to incorporate some logic around how or when that version was created. For example, do you save a new version every five minutes, or every hour, or every day, or on every data change or on every ten changes and so on? You'll need to have a way of naming these files that supports this method so it's clear which saved file you're looking at.

Of course, the more often you save your file (i.e. create a new version), the more granular your ability to understand data changes as they happened. However, this creates many more files than saving less frequently. This larger number of files will still need to have a meaningful name that clearly identifies it in the context of the versioning scheme.

If saving frequently with the correspondingly complex naming scheme sounds like too much work, and saving maybe once per hour or even once per day would make life easier, consider this. The most valuable information you'll typically work on is the most recent. If you couldn't recover a day's work from five years ago, you might not care that much. However if you lost all of today's work you'd probably be furious! So there's a strong argument for saving your work more frequently to avoid this kind of stress. But as we have seen, more frequent saves = more files = more complex method for organising and saving them.

Which brings us back to the concept of a naming convention. It's simply a well defined, logical, consistent set of rules for naming a file that can accommodate larger but otherwise unknown amounts of data in the future. If you're going to use individual files to create and store your work, it's crucial that you store them in a way that's operationally useful and the data they contain is adequately protected.

One last point on saving files, and as you might expect I've saved the worst for last.

If you are creating multiple versions of your file(s) to enable an audit trail for data integrity and quality purposes, it's quite likely that the save location or folder will form part of the naming convention. After all, there is a limit on how long the name of a file can be so it may be that for your operational needs you need to create a set of folders, (also with meaningful names) to simplify file naming or at least keep the name within certain limits.

One characteristic of general purpose software is that, by definition it can't know where you want to save any given file. It will probably have a default save location which can be anywhere you like, however if you are relying on a logical folder structure to help you manage your file versions, then you're going to need to save in some other place than the default location pretty much every time. This takes us back to whether you have automatic saves enabled or not. If you have automatic saves enabled for safety, then your file will very likely be saved in the wrong place every time. If, on the other hand you decide that automatic saves are more trouble than they're worth, then you're now reliant on remembering to save your file in the correct manner (every change, every 5 mins etc.?) AND in the correct location. This may be easy and error free at 9am on a Monday, but can you guarantee the same for 3pm on a Friday? Every single time?

So let's assume you have created a file naming convention and a corresponding storage plan and you have accepted that none of this is perfect but it's good enough. Problem solved, right?

Oh dear me no, not by a long shot.

So far we've only looked at files created by, and for the working benefit of a single person. What about sharing that information with others? After all, we tend to work in teams and teams need to collaborate which typically means sharing the information they're working with.

Having created a file with all the above operational requirements taken into account, how are you going to share this information? If you thought it was as simple as getting the IT guys to make the file shareable from your PC, well technically you could but as we'll see you absolutely shouldn't.

To begin with, we need to take a quick dive into the world of permissions. Permissions is the catch all term to describe who is allowed to do what with information.

Now in order to hand out permissions to people, i.e. to allow them to work with your precious data, first you need to know who they are. In the same way you wouldn't hand your house keys over to the first stranger you met on the street, you probably won't want to make your data available to just anyone. After all, business data has value and in most cases that value is extremely high. So you need some way of making sure that only the right people can access your files and to do that you need a comprehensive list of everyone who could conceivably want access so you can decide individually whether to grant it or not.

To hold that list on your PC would be cumbersome, and when I say cumbersome I mean completely and utterly unworkable. The chances of your PC being the only one in the organisation that might need to share information is pretty low, and the prospect of creating and maintaining a list of everyone in the business on each PC creates huge issues.

So in order to grant permissions effectively, you're going to need a central list of people and someone to keep it up to date. That way, everybody who wants to share a file can refer to the same set of people. If this list can't be stored on your PC, where can it be stored? If it's in some central location then the responsibility for maintaining and updating it will probably lie with someone else.

In case it's not clear, this is absolutely a management issue not a technical one. We're still talking about how business tasks are completed, and it's only the complication around managing and protecting access to critical data that means some additional technical skill is needed, i.e. an IT function.

Let's look at ways to centrally manage identities and permissions.

It turns out there's some good news here. There are a couple of solutions that can achieve this at an affordable price. At time of writing, both Microsoft 365 and Google Workspace have elegant built in tools for identity management and security. While the configuration and maintenance of these tools lies very much in the realm of the technical expert, the huge business advantage here is they can be purchased on a highly granular basis, i.e. per user.

But hang on, we're not out of the woods yet. Creating permissions is only part of the story. Where are we going to store our precious files so that everybody who's allowed to can access them? Obviously it needs to be some kind of centralised storage that is available all the time. If a critical file suddenly disappeared because Brian turned his PC off to go for lunch, then that file isn't as useful as it needs to be.

We need some kind of centralised storage space for shared files. That storage space needs to be available whenever anyone needs it, and since that demand is unpredictable, 24/7 availability is the only way to ensure it's met. It also needs to be accessible from wherever your people are doing their work. If everyone works in a single office, then that requirement looks very different to one that meets the needs of a fully mobile or widely distributed team.

OK, to be on the safe side and sure everyone can access their files from anywhere, we'll use one of the Internet based file storage services. Simple! Well, once again, not quite. Before we can start uploading files, we need to make sure that our chosen storage service can work with our user management system. Understanding exactly whether and how this works is way beyond the capability of a non technical business leader.

I've come a long way to make a very important point.

The point is not that these things are easy or hard, it's simply that they can't be ignored or overlooked from business management level. While you can delegate the technical aspects of implementation and ongoing maintenance, the responsibility for making sure your business has effective tools for workflow management lies with you.

Where general purpose software scores highly is where its ability to do pretty much anything reasonably intuitively or without much training is a big advantage. Any tool that's easy to use is probably going to be quick to use as well, which makes it ideal for jobs you don't have to do over and over again. One off tasks, anything that doesn't need to fit into a repeatable process, these kinds of activity are well suited to programs such as these. However, these advantages do not make up for the fact that overall, general purpose software is absolutely the wrong tool set for workflow management.

I'm going to close out this section with one last observation.

Having gone to some lengths to show that general purpose software is not the right tool for mature or growing businesses, Microsoft 365 or Google Business are actually great options for businesses of up to a few hundred people. This is nothing to do with their included general purpose programs, but because of their ability to centrally manage your user security and permissions to a high standard at a reasonable price. What this means is that you can more or less ignore the software programs included with both and still get great value from them!

The next category is Task Aware software.

TASK AWARE

Task Aware software is the next step up in business utility, in that it has some 'understanding' of the underlying logic around the information it handles. A good example would be a finance package such as Sage, Xero or QuickBooks.

When working with titles like these, they have a set of rules around business accounting built right in. They 'understand' that this value relates to an income amount, that value to an asset and the other one to a depreciation value.

Therefore we can reasonably say that a finance package is 'aware' of the finance function, or that it is Task Aware.

It's worth thinking about this in a little more depth.

To begin with, the included logic or rule set has the benefit of some measure of error protection. For example, if you need to track some proportion of your income for sales tax purposes, the software will already know what tax regime you are working in and can allocate these amounts automatically. There will be many examples of this kind of logic throughout the package.

What I'm highlighting here is the first example of business process automation in software. Your business has a requirement to track sales tax, and it needs to happen with every sale. Tracking sales tax is a process, and the software we have chosen automates this for us.

But wait, there's more!

On the basis that your finance software understands

the rules of business finance, and contains records of all your transactions, it is ideally placed to report on those transactions in the context of the rules you need to follow. So your purchase of this software has delivered two extremely valuable benefits. You have automated a meaningful part of your business, and in such a way that your management team can quickly understand how that part of the business is performing.

OK this sounds awesome, is this a trick can I repeat for other parts of my business? Well absolutely yes you can. You will find task aware software available for marketing, sales, projects, supply chain, inventory, H&S, HR, warranty etc. the list is almost endless.

So we're home and dry. Task aware software is all we'll ever need right?

Well no, not quite. There are, as you may have guessed, some limitations and drawbacks.

Firstly, task aware software is not useful 'out of the box'. It will require some amount of configuration to accurately reflect your business and your trading conditions and environment. This configuration work needs to be accounted for in the software budgeting stage. You may be offered configuration services as an option when purchasing software, and you need to balance this cash cost against the operational cost of using your own people to carry out this work.

Which leads me on to the next consideration, training.

Task aware software, while as intuitive as the vendor can make it, will need some user training before it becomes useful. How much training depends on the complexity and ease of use of the software, plus the aptitude, experience and willingness of your team to learn. In particular, if you are going to get your own people to carry out the configuration work, they will need rather more training (to 'Super User' level) than the rest of the team. This again needs to be budgeted for.

There is another limitation to take on board, and I've saved the best for last. To be sure, it's a very limited and specific interpretation of the word 'best', but here we are.

Where task aware software runs out of steam is right there in the name. It's aware of a limited set of tasks, as opposed to the end to end set that makes up your business in its entirety. If we take the example of a sales management software package, it may not know where new sales leads come from, nor indeed what happens to closed sales that go off for some kind of fulfilment or other. It is undisputed master of its domain, but that domain has clear and well defined limits. Even our dazzling finance package which for obvious reasons knows a lot about your business, may not know anything about your employees beyond their salary costs, that responsibility is handled by your HR management software, which in turn probably won't know about each employees safety record and so on.

So from a great start into the world of process automation and management reporting, we've hit a bit of a bump. Do we have to live with a set of business information islands with no bridges between them?

Actually no. Sighs of relief all round!

There is a solution but it's not perfect. Commercial software vendors, being the clever and resourceful people they are, have thought of this and have equipped their product (in most cases) with a data exchange capability called an API that lets them communicate in a meaningful way with other software packages. The trick here is making a specific pair of APIs talk seamlessly and there is enough complexity around that to pause the topic here. Suffice to say it can be done with some limitations, but how that happens is best left to your software vendor or technology support partner.

So where does this leave us? We know that general purpose software is cheap and easy to use but a waking nightmare for process automation purposes. We have discovered that task aware software solves these problems, but at a financial and operational cost and with the added complexity of having multiple packages to work with.

Wouldn't it be lovely if there was a way to take all that process automation and reporting goodness and smooth out all the multi package / interface issues we looked at? Oddly enough, there is. OK, it's not actually that odd since I set up these categories myself but let's not dwell. It's time to meet category three - business aware software.

BUSINESS AWARE

Business aware software takes all the best bits of task aware software and kicks it into the stratosphere. Here's how it does it.

Business aware software is an 'end to end' (or 'soup to nuts' as my Australian colleagues like to put it) solution for business process automation. It works on the basis that it automates all or at least the vast majority of your business in a single piece of software. In other words, one working environment to handle all the steps on the customer journey, plus the supporting back office functions.

Let's look at the advantages first.

The big one, by which I mean the really big one is that software in this category understands the underlying logic of your whole business. Specifically, it has been built around the typical workflow of your industry. As you can see, this makes it highly specialised but at the same time uniquely well suited to the tasks you need to complete every day.

So sales tasks naturally resolve into service delivery tasks (whatever that looks like in your industry) which consequently resolve into billing tasks and so on, right the way through your business. Let's drill down into a single example task to understand just how powerful this is in business terms.

Suppose a sale has just been closed for a product that requires delivery and on site assembly, and you now need to complete that piece of the process so you can bill the customer.

What do you need to know in order for this customer to receive their finished product?

- Who the customer is
- Where they are
- What they bought
- When it's needed

What else?

- Where is this product in your inventory?
- What is the current stock level?
- Do any of the items have a limited shelf life?

- Do you need to order any further items or components?
- Do any of these need provenance or source evidence tracking?
- When will these additional items arrive? Do they have an assigned location for storage?
- Is any sub assembly required?
- If so, where will this happen? Who will do it and when?
- Who is going to deliver this product?
- Will they assemble it as well?
- How many people does delivery and assembly need?
- Do they have the right skills, training and supervision?
- What other equipment will they need on site?
- Has a site survey and risk assessment been carried out?
- Does their availability match up with the agreed delivery date?

The list could go on a lot further, but I'm just illustrating that for something simple in principle like selling and delivering a product needs a lot of supporting activity.

Which of these two scenarios sounds better to you?

Scenario 1

You have one or more people in marketing, sales, supply chain, field service, finance, HR, H&S, etc. each of whom maintains their own records relating to their business function. For each sale or project, you have a series of meetings where everybody reports their progress updates and any issues or blockers. It's only at these meetings that something approaching a true representation of readiness can be obtained, but they are also the point at which problems become apparent. This inevitably leads to lengthy discussions on why your service delivery position might not be in the state it should be.

Imagine;

Sales has handed a closed deal to service delivery, and an expectation of revenue to finance. However, they hadn't checked that the customer's expectations around delivery could be met, or they had confirmed that the stock was available but had no way of knowing whether the people needed for on site assembly were on leave or otherwise unavailable. Meanwhile, HR have implemented a much needed and long awaited skills and professional development framework and have finally been able to put some structure around the overall ability level of the whole business team. They are now able to clarify whether a team member (in our case the site assembly team) has the appropriate training for the job at hand, however sharing that information is not easy so service delivery management can't be sure that they are sending the right people.

While this is occurring, the post sale / warranty team have highlighted an urgent, widespread product issue that means further on site assembly work needs to be halted while investigations are carried out and a remedy plan is created.

I could go on, however the important point here is that even though everyone across the business is carrying out their work to the best of their ability and trying to take the needs of other teams into account, information lives in silos and cross functional collaboration is not instant. These and a thousand similar examples will inevitably arise. Quite apart from the damage this will do to internal relationships, most importantly the poor customer ends up with a terrible experience!

Now, suppose you had something like the following:

Scenario 2

Your sales system wasn't able to confirm a delivery / install date with the customer until all the supply chain, inventory and logistics requirements were met. In turn, the state and readiness of all those resources was automatically tracked in real time such that this data was available to whoever needed it. So when speaking to the customer, your sales team was able to give up to date, factually accurate information regarding their delivery and even update it later should the situation change.

At this point you may be thinking "yes that's all very well, but our business is nowhere near that big or complex so we don't need an elegant, expensive piece of software to manage it"

That may be true today, but I invite you to consider the following; do you want to be in exactly the same place tomorrow as you are today? How about this time next year? How about three years time? The point is, either you are aiming for growth or you're not. If you are, then do you really want to wait until you are drowning in bad process and poor customer outcomes or do you choose to accept that complexity is an inevitable function of business growth so planning for it is the sensible thing to do?

Now before we go off the deep end and try to buy the first piece of enterprise software we come across, there are some crucial factors to take into account.

- Process maturity
- Functionality and feature requirements
- Learning curve and end user adoption
- Project management
- Overall price versus value

Process maturity

Before any project can be undertaken to implement enterprise software, it is critically important to make sure the processes within your business are both well understood and well documented. By well understood, I mean that each functional lead such as marketing, sales, finance etc. doesn't just understand how their own processes are executed and why it's done that way, but also how all the other functions are performed as well. We have already seen how huge problems can arise from limited understanding of different areas of the business, so a high degree of mutual insight is key to success in deployment.

Assuming that your process set is well understood across the business, it is absolutely required that it is captured in a comprehensive and consistent way. One of the reasons enterprise software is as useful as it is, is that it allows you great freedom to implement the way you run your business as you see fit. While that's wonderful in principle, it means you have to make a large number of operational policy decisions when configuring the software itself. If you have a comprehensive, widely understood, consistently described set of processes, then the configuration process will go fairly smoothly. If you don't, then this part will involve a lot of (probably heated) discussion around why various tasks are carried out the way they are. This is both depressing and avoidable.

Learning curve and end user adoption

OK, there's no way past this one. Complex software takes a while for everyone to learn and even longer to get comfortable with, and ignoring this will jeopardise the project. There are two inter related factors at play here, I'll describe them separately but they should really be considered aspects of the same thing.

Your users will need training. Pretty obvious, right? Well yes but we need to dig a little deeper to understand what's going on in the user community.

When a management team, for well researched and thoroughly justified reasons, announce that there is going to be a major software project and new ways of doing things, the way it is received by staff is very different than the way it was intended. You see, the very set of conditions that have highlighted the need for a comprehensive software solution, are also the ones that have been developed by trial and error (and you would hope with the best intentions) by your team over an extended period. In other words, your people are being asked to embrace the prospect of new ways of doing everything, with systems they've never seen before while having their existing methods and practices removed - all while being required to deliver the same amount of work as they are today.

I cannot over emphasise how unpalatable and distressing this proposal can be, even though the eventual benefits to the team far outweigh the inconvenience incurred in implementation.

What does reluctance this look like in practical terms?

There is an excellent book on the subject called Our

Iceberg Is Melting written by John Kotter which covers how people deal with critical change, however in my own experience, you'll find any combination of:

The doomsayers; *"it'll never work."* - these people, having publicly invested in this position, will put effort into making sure this comes true as often as not

The local experts; *"management knows nothing about how things happen on a daily basis, they're not qualified to tell us anything."*

The genuinely terrified; *"I'm no good with technology, what if it's too complicated / I make a mistake / I break it?"*

The knowledge is power people; *"I've spent years creating this spreadsheet, it's critical to the business and I'm the only one who knows how it works which puts me in a position of influence."*

The local workaround crew; *"I'll nod and smile and not make any waves but I'll keep using my old spreadsheets to manage my work and just enter the results into the new system."*

You can see from this limited sample that the people management aspects of what looked like a purely technical project are at least as important as the technology itself if not more so!

So you have two challenges to meet here, the first one being making sure your team have all the training they need, together with assessments and followups for learning gaps. The second is to make sure your people are engaged with the new way of doing things and performing their tasks. While you can expect much of the learning delivery to come from the vendor, how are you going to ensure that learning is applied in practice?

If your change leaders were already operational experts, well versed in how the business really operates on a daily basis and regularly consulted by other members of staff, and they shared your vision of a smoother operating, less stressful working environment, then they will become both evangelists for the new way of working as well as being able to make effective changes in the system should local conditions need it.

It is also common for such Super Users to either lead the team training effort or pick up after the vendor training has taken place, using real world examples of how individual tasks are completed.

Finally, your Super Users are evangelists for the system and its benefits. Already trusted by the rest of the team, their view of how the working world will be improved will carry a lot more weight than senior management.

Now you may be thinking, hang on a moment. This sounds like a lot of work, my supervisors are already working flat out and don't have time to take on anything more. Unfortunately, there's no easy option here. You need your best, most experienced people to be system Super Users and help drive effective change. The criticality of this work should not be underestimated either. You need to be thinking of allocating at least 50% of their time to Super User work, certainly as the software launch gets closer.

You could look at this as an opportunity to give someone else in the team a chance to work at a more senior level and pick up some of the work your supervisory expert has been solely responsible for up to now.

So what does this different approach look like to your

potentially reluctant user base? In order:

The doomsayers will be required to justify their negative position in front of someone who's probably more experienced and is already invested in the success of the project. It's the same for the 'management knows nothing' faction. Their objections will need to survive the scrutiny of a genuine local expert. The genuinely worried will have local resource to both reassure and provide additional support if needed, and the local workaround users will more easily be able to see how their work will be easier when new methods are adopted.

This does leave anyone invested in knowledge being power as a problem. Regardless of how else they present their objections, i.e. as any of the previous types, their motivations are not the best. However, at this point anyone not on board with the overall benefits will start to become obvious and their arguments won't stand up to much scrutiny. This is the point where a software deployment issue becomes a separate management one and can be referred to HR for further review.

Project Management

While Super Users bring immense value to the software roll out process, they are operational experts first and foremost and it is a mistake to try to dilute that value by tasking them with any additional project management oversight or responsibility.

I don't want to dive too deeply into the world of project management, it's a rich and complex subject about which many great books have been written. Per the enduring theme of this book however, I do want to explore the 'why' rather than the 'how'.

Two questions need answering before we can continue. What value does project management add to our software implementation, and who should do it?

To address the first question, it's best to think of project management as an active form of risk management. If your shiny new enterprise software system is intended to run your whole business for the foreseeable future, then it absolutely has to work as expected and deliver every last one of the required benefits. Consider what not achieving this would look like. You have identified operational and management pain that is impacting both your ability to execute on a daily basis and preventing effective, forward looking management decision making. If your future success is deemed to rely on solving these pain points, and they are not solved, then by definition your future is at risk.

Project management is one of the measures you can take to make sure that everyone's expectations are captured, understood, incorporated and delivered.

What level of expertise you need in the PM role will vary depending on the size, activity volume, maturity and complexity of your business together with the anticipated scope of the software itself. Your operational horizon also has an impact here. If your new software is only expected to last you two years before you anticipate outgrowing it and you are OK with the prospect of replacing it then your estimates around its performance will only need to last as long. We have already seen that the hardest management decisions to make are the ones with the most distant horizon, less distant ones or in particular ones with a known validity are at least somewhat easier. However, as is more typical with 'business aware' software, the anticipated lifetime is less clear while the expected benefits are expected to remain more or less indefinitely.

To summarise, if you have a new, fairly simple business with low transaction volume, then your project management requirements will be different to those needed for a well established larger enterprise. The larger and more mature your business, the greater your need for professional project management expertise. If you don't have that skill set in your team already you'll need to outsource.

In closing, I'd strongly advise including your technology partner at the earliest stages, not least because software project management may be a service they can provide.

Price versus value

One attribute of enterprise software that tends to negatively impact adoption is price. Whichever way you slice it, this stuff is not cheap. In fact, back in the days when having a server in your building was the only way to enjoy the benefits of business aware software, the hardware costs contributed massively to the overall cost of deployment.

One reason this made life difficult for the finance team was in calculating the true cost picture to offset the expected benefits. As we'll see a bit later, computer servers have a host of attendant costs that are hard to attribute to the software project. For example, you have already gone to the expense of installing a server in your building, and then add another one to run your new software that utilises some of the same infrastructure such as power and air conditioning. Does the new server incur some of the infrastructure cost of the original one? If so, how does that affect the financial reporting around the original asset? Has it become mysteriously cheaper for accounting purposes even though nothing has actually changed? If not, is the true cost of the new server being artificially lowered due to its supporting infrastructure being accounted for elsewhere? While these might seem arbitrary concerns with little impact outside the finance team, they have real implications when calculating ROI on your software spend.

But that was then, this is now. As we already know, modern software is available on a 'per license' model which delivers huge advantages when estimating price versus value.

Before we move on, I want to make sure the management implications of 'per license' software delivery are clear. When trying to understand the overall cost burden of any new software solution, the temptation is to roll up the combined costs of all the licenses you need and project forward over some period of years. The best you will achieve with this method is palpitations and the desire for a soothing drink! You see, while the overall cost has some importance, it is nowhere near as significant as cashflow.

Effectively 'renting' your software on a per person per month basis enables you to do two extremely valuable things. Firstly it keeps the maximum amount of cash in your business as there are no nasty CapEx spikes associated with server installations and so on. Secondly, and even more importantly, the per head cost model allows you to apportion your software costs to your other staff overheads instead of some centralised technology budget. This is transformational stuff.

All of a sudden, the cost of the tools someone needs to do their job can be allocated directly to them which means you can accurately model the true costs of growing your business in the most granular possible way. "For every new staff member I take on in the future, I can accurately predict the full set of associated costs, and track that cost directly back to productivity."

OK so we have some cost management advantages. What about the operational benefits?

Well this is the most visible bit, and while everything we're about to cover also applies to task aware software, we're going to focus on the example at hand, business aware software.

Harking back to our earlier section on the Productive Hour, we already know that the biggest productivity gains are to be found in tasks that happen predictably and repeatedly i.e. our nominal 80% of routine tasks. Although the days of the time and motion study are thankfully a long way behind us, it is worth understanding how long it currently takes each of your team to carry out each of their given tasks.

Let me clear about this - where a task doesn't require judgement or approval of some description and simply moves a piece of information further long its associated workflow, then the prospect is that once implemented in software that task will take no time at all! In other words, with the right software in place your team will be fully engaged in work that directly impacts the quality of whatever it is you do, and the rest of their work will become instantaneous.

At this point, it's over to you to calculate what that efficiency bonus is, and how much it moves the salary multiplier we looked at before. Once this number has been revealed, the comparison with the cost of the software itself (factoring in all the implementation costs over your chosen ROI period of course!) becomes clearer. This is why trying to get a handle on costs versus benefits is not best achieved by rolling up the costs and trying to guess what the positive outcomes might be.

So where have we got to when considering Business Aware software?

We now know it has:

- End to end business logic baked in
- Seamless process automation opportunities
- High complexity and significant adoption hurdles
- Very high ROI benefits

So Business Aware represents something of a high risk / high reward way forward. Is there anything else it has to offer that might make it additionally attractive? As it turns out, yes. There are a couple of extra attributes that make it a compelling option even for small businesses.

The first is scalability.

If you have ambitious growth goals for your enterprise, then one thing you really want is the smoothest possible path to get there. As we have already seen, migrating between workflow management tools is likely to cause huge disruption so you might want to avoid it if possible. One of the main characteristics of business aware software is its suitability for large organisations. Flexibility that just looks like unneeded complication at the scale of a new venture will pay huge dividends as your business grows and its inherent complexity inevitably grows with it. That's when the ability to apply very fine grained controls over how your business runs without needing to halt and install a new process management system pays out massively. So even though enterprise grade software will feel like overkill in the early stages, (and if you weren't going to grow then it would be), it's actually a smart long term bet.

The next relates to best practice.

We'll look at this again in the next section, however I would invite you to consider the following:

Can you solemnly promise that the way you conduct your business operations is absolutely, 100% solid gold guaranteed, cross your heart and hope to die the best it could possibly be? Is there nothing at all you could learn from others in your industry? To put it another way, is running successfully enough? Or are you open to finding ways to turn good into great?

One of the less obvious attributes of business aware software is how its own growth benefits its customers.

You see, business software companies are in competition with each other just like any other business. They all know that making their software more useful will win them sales while lagging behind will cost them dearly. So they are all powerfully motivated to stay at the cutting edge of functionality.

That's fine, but how do they know what the cutting edge actually looks like? This happens in two ways at the same time. Firstly, they use insight gained from how businesses typically use their software day to day, and turn this insight into new features. These new features are added to the development plan for the software to form what's known as a development roadmap. They also receive requests from their customers - that's you by the way! - for features that would solve specific local problems or make their business run a bit better. Now the interesting thing about feature requests is that some of those requested features might actually improve the product for all their customers not just the one requesting them. So by combining product roadmap features with the best of those requested from the customer base, the software vendor can actually end up with a product that embodies best practice from right across your industry.

What all of the above means, is that while you can and should carefully model your own processes with a view to implementing them in software, you may also benefit from adopting the default or preferred methods in the software itself. Per my point above, unless you are 100% confident that your way of doing things is the best possible in your industry and couldn't imaginably be improved, then being open to methods suggested by your software vendor may improve your business without any additional cost. Of course, that's not in any way guaranteed, but it's an potentially interesting way to improve your operational maturity through the learnings of others.

To close out the section on software, let's look at bespoke or custom solutions.

BESPOKE SOLUTIONS

To begin with, what are the benefits of having software written specifically for you?

Well most obviously, you will end up with an operating

environment that is fine tuned for your business and its operating model. You don't have to make any compromises or bend your way of doing things to accommodate how the rest of your industry does them. To address the challenge I raised above, if you are absolutely convinced that your business operations are both unique and as well managed as they can possibly be, then bespoke software may be an option for you.

Now there are many areas in your business where truly bespoke software could be a benefit, but I'll take the two most common ones as examples.

To begin with, where your business runs on a mix of task aware software, you'll find that the built in interfaces between them often lack flexibility. Typically these interfaces are based on matching values such as names, addresses, sale amounts and similar to their nearest equivalent in the next piece of software. On the one hand this makes sense since we're talking about business software so different titles ought to have something in common, but then again there is an extraordinarily large number of possible combinations of different software packages so it's extremely difficult for each vendor to guarantee that their API is 100% compatible with every other.

If you bump into a situation where inherent limitations in interface mapping mean two pieces of software you absolutely rely on can't work effectively, then you may need to get a custom interface written for you.

At the other end of the scale in business aware software, if you find after extensive research and much software testing, that none of the packages available do what you need, then having a bespoke end to end software solution built for you may be your only way forward.

Before we progress, I should draw an important distinction here. For reasons of convenience, I'm going to talk about two different kinds of custom enterprise software as if they were the same thing. The first kind is where a software vendor sits down with the proverbial blank sheet and starts writing entirely new code based on your stated requirements.

The second kind is where a software vendor starts with a 'plain vanilla' cloud based solution such as Microsoft Dynamics or Oracle ERP or SAP (there are many others) and adapts them according to your needs. Industry buzz word alert, ERP stands for Enterprise Resource Planning and is a class of software rather than something more specific. You'll also likely run across MRP in your research, where the M stands for Manufacturing. Trip right off the tongue, don't they, so glad we have these logical and intuitive acronyms to rely on!

To be absolutely clear, these are wildly different ways of achieving a given outcome. However, for my purposes I'm going to treat them as equivalent as they have some significant attributes in common for the points I need to make.

We've established that having software written just for you will result in a tightly focused end result, optimised for your business and nobody else's. No compromises has to equal a better outcome, right?

Well yes, but only under ideal conditions.

To begin with, it's reasonable to want to compare costs against the other alternatives available to you. The first challenge you're going to hit on the bespoke software road to nirvana is how much you're going to have to pay. This is actually a little tricky because whoever is proposing to write this stuff for you needs to know they're not going to lose money on their work so they need to be sure how much work is involved. The reason this is harder then it first appears is because the set of requirements you give them is unlikely to be perfect or complete. If either of these turns out to be true (both is not uncommon!) then the software author has to adjust what they are doing to accommodate and it's impossible to tell in advance how much work that adjustment will take. As you can guess, extra work equals extra cost, and that cost has to be accommodated somewhere.

This can be resolved in one of two ways. Either the vendor will guarantee an outcome, i.e. they will keep working away until you are happy with what they have produced, or they will guarantee a price for a given amount of development effort, quite possibly expressed in days. As you can see, neither of these methods is ideal, at least from your point of view. What you really wanted was a known outcome for an agreed price, but that's not how things work in this environment.

What will probably happen is that your vendor will agree a price for your initial set of requirements, with any adds or changes priced additionally subject to approval.

However, we shouldn't get hung up on the first obstacle we come across. We want to understand what the full experience looks like. So let's proceed!

The next thing to take into account is copyright or intellectual property rights. Why might this be a concern?

When you set out to have a custom piece of software written for your business, it'll almost certainly be on the basis of a very high degree of expertise in your industry or service. You'll have researched a number of other software options before deciding that bespoke was the way to go, which means that your software is highly specialised.

Now much as we all want to believe we are radical innovators, bravely carving a wholly new trail through the business landscape, the reality is probably somewhat different. Compared to the number of businesses starting up in existing markets, the volume of true innovators is low.

However, if you are indeed one of these rare and magical beasts, and you have created a completely new way of servicing a previously undefined market, then you're likely to find copycat businesses rapidly following in your footsteps. While there's not much you can do about that, if you have developed a unique software solution to automate the delivery of whatever that market requires then it's at least possible you could make some extra income by turning your software into a product in its own right.

Great! A way of recouping some of your software investment! Well yes, but only if you have agreed in advance that you own the intellectual property in that software, i.e. the right sell it as your own. You may find that this is part of your software vendor's standard terms but it's absolutely something to be aware of before a single line of code is crafted on your behalf.

To close out this topic, if you do find yourself in the position of market leader in a brand new rapidly growing industry sector but aren't thrilled about the distraction of trying to take your unique software to market yourself, you might be able to agree a joint venture with a software author such that they provide the development and sales expertise and you provide the industry knowledge and workflow insight. After all, every single piece of business software available was originally created through a combination of industry expertise and software development skill. You could be next!

There is one more crucially important point to take on board when contemplating custom software, and that's ongoing development and maintenance.

Let's suppose your original set of requirements were met at an acceptable cost, and your new software environment is doing everything you hoped it would. Your efficiency is through the roof, your customers love you, it's been a great outcome. You can now concentrate on growth.

Now whatever else growth means to you, by definition it also means change. To grow is to become different, even if that difference is simply being more of what you were before. As we have already discovered in the section on process automation, just doing more of the same thing increases the volume of edge cases and escalations even if the proportions stay the same. So tomorrow already looks different to today, and it's not hard to imagine that more challenging changes than simple linear growth will come along.

The question here is, what does your software need to do differently to cope with or adjust to new trading conditions? What operating parameters have to be invented to keep you ahead of the change curve? You can see that this isn't just likely but pretty much inevitable.

Let's wind back to your original set of requirements. These were based on your best understanding of your business as it runs today, combined with your best guess of what the future looked like. As we already know, your best guess is based on one or more supporting assumptions and regardless of the amount of data and management reporting available to you your assumptions won't be perfect.

What I'm getting at here, is that the initial iteration of your business management software is almost certain not to be the last. Opportunities and threats will arise, unforeseen and unforeseeable circumstances will bite you if given the chance. Since your software system is effectively all that stands between you and chaos, you're going to need to adapt it over time.

This raises some profound points.

Did you agree with your software vendor what your terms might be for further development? How much will they charge you for further work? If your relationship was pretty positive through the original development and delivery phase, they may be inclined to keep their prices reasonable when quoting for further work. However, this is a long way outside your control and so can't be guaranteed.

If it's starting to feel like you're in a difficult position, then you'd be right. You only have one software vendor, and you rely on them absolutely for the performance and future proofing of your business.

At this point you may think "well there's plenty of other software writers out there, they were battering my door down when I was originally looking for a vendor, I'll just get one of them to take over development". This is another of those propositions that sounds simple in principle but turns out (surprise surprise!) to be a lot harder in practice.

The reason here is that different software vendors have different ways of documenting what they've done, why it was done and why it was done in that particular way. If you have a team of people working on a single project, it's crucial that effective documentation is written and maintained. If you were to ask a software vendor to pick up a project written by someone else, it may have high quality documentation but then again it might not have. So their first concern will be how the risks associated with quality and delivery could affect them. You will find their pricing reflects this!

To be clear, I am not suggesting that bespoke software is a bad idea. There are many outstandingly clever vendors out there who may be able to provide you with a business management solution that's 100% perfect for your needs. I'm simply highlighting that there are management issues involved that fall outside the scope of technology and software functionality and these should absolutely be taken into account in the decision making process.

BUSINESS REPORTING

So we now know that the right software will enable your processes to run at max efficiency, making your people significantly more productive by allowing them to play to their strengths.

That's fine, but where's the direct management benefit? After all this is a book about decision making, and we know that decisions and their corresponding assumptions need supporting information.

Let's look at business decisions in a little more detail before proceeding.

If I asked you to make an operational decision right now that had an impact in 24 hours, you probably wouldn't struggle much. For example, if one member of staff had gone sick and you needed someone else to cover for them tomorrow, working out who to call probably wouldn't be that difficult. Obviously I'm ignoring the number of people you have and the amount of flexibility around bringing people in, the point here is that deciding what to do is not that hard.

There are two reasons for this.

The first is that because tomorrow usually looks very much like today, you can consider the decision in isolation. In our example, someone going sick is considered the only material change between today and tomorrow so you can treat the issue as having no other impacts.

The other factor at play here also relies on tomorrow looking like today. It means that you feel you can hold all the information needed to make that decision in your head at one time.

As you can see, while the assumption that tomorrow is the same as today is comparatively safe simply because things don't usually change that fast in a business, it's not 100% safe. Tomorrow is not the same as today, however similar it is.

The point is, this assumption becomes less and less safe as tomorrow becomes next week, then next month, then next quarter and so on. What we're looking at here is a sliding scale of decision making complexity combined with outcome risk. Today's decisions about tomorrow are reasonably simple and therefore appear to have comparatively limited scope, but as the decision horizon gets further and further away from you, your ability to hold all the required information in your head becomes harder and the number of variables increases which means the likelihood of making an error goes up.

Incidentally, this is why it's not uncommon for business owners and managers to end up deferring long term 'hard' decisions in favour of a continued stream of short term ones. If you've ever found yourself in that position, you'll recognise the scenario.

This problem was alluded to in the introduction to this book. We found our intrepid travellers in an awkward spot simply because a succession of small changes had been adopted as inconsequential, which ultimately left them in a position where they didn't have enough information to make a critical decision and each subsequent option available looked as good as any other.

What this shows is that even though some decisions can be considered low risk, low does not equal zero risk. Using an approximation such as tomorrow being the same as today to base your decisions on has inherent risk simply because it's not actually true. A sequence of decisions based on similar approximations can leave you wildly adrift even if each one was only a little off.

We have a challenge here. To avoid the attendant risks above, we need to condense enough accurate, up to date information into easy to digest forms to help our decision making process. What kind of information will we need?

- What's happening right now
- What's been happening up to this point
- What's likely to happen in the future

With this information, we can start to compare with our original expectations (our business plan!) to see where the differences lie and decide what actions are appropriate.

At this point, I'm going to introduce some new terms, dashboards, reports and forecasts. Although these probably won't be completely new to you, I want to take a moment to make sure the differences are clear.

To begin with, all of these are strictly speaking, reports. When we talk about management reporting, it's a catch all term for extracting summary information from business systems. However, for our purposes I will create some distinctions to make things easier as we move forward.

We already know that all the information relating to business operations exists in our software systems, simply because that's what such systems create and consume.

So what information should be available to us?

- What we expected to be true (our plan)
- What's happening right now (dashboards)
- What's been happening up to this point (reports)
- What's likely to happen in the future (forecasts)

Let's create an example, and refer back to the decision making scenario we examined at the beginning of this chapter. What about our manager who's tasked with finding a replacement for someone who has gone sick?

If they could have a visual representation of who was on leave right now, or away on training, or who had just finished a night shift and so on, they wouldn't need to rely on their own interpretation which may be flawed or just out of date. In other words, a single dashboard with a summary of availability would improve the whole process.

Now let's think about the next management meeting. It's likely that the team will want to know more about availability trends in staffing, to see if there might be other factors impacting sickness levels. Are more people going sick on Fridays or Mondays or the days immediately before or after public holidays? Are there outliers such as people who never go sick or are off way more than the average? The question is of course, what can we learn from this information?

As such questions become more nuanced or wider in scope, more information is needed to extract meaning so the presentation format will necessarily be more complex. This where a management report would be required from your business data. Please keep in mind, the intent of a report is exactly the same as a dashboard. To collate and present enough information to make a decision in the simplest possible format.

If a dashboard tells us what's happening right now, and a report helps us to understand why, then the next logical thing to want to know is what would the future look like if known trends continued. This is where we need a forecast.

As you can see, a forecast is by necessity based on a number of assumptions, the biggest of which is that all relevant data has been included and that known or anticipated trends continue. So long as these assumptions are recognised as such, then a forecast is very useful for illustrating 'what if' scenarios.

Using these tools, we can ask ourselves some meaningful questions:

- Do we understand the reasons why there is a difference between our expectations and reality?
- Do those reasons highlight a fault in our assumptions or our original data?
- Should we use the difference between what we expected and what we actually find to bring us back to our original plan or as supporting information to change it?
- Based on all the above, what we might expect to be true in the future?
- If that future is not where we want to go, what do we need to do right now to change it?

These are absolutely business critical questions. Typically complex, opaque, uncertain and fiendishly difficult questions, but still crucial for the long term survival and success of the business.

Incidentally, this is where your leadership team adds a lot of value. While they are doubtless experts in their operational responsibilities such as human resources or finance, their evidence based contributions to critical future facing decisions is their most valuable activity. If, on the other hand, you are your leadership team, then this task is all the harder. As I mentioned earlier, there is a temptation to concentrate on short term limited scope decisions that one person can reasonably make. However as I hope is now clear, this is very much a false comfort and your resulting business journey may leave you in an unexpected place.

So what information do you need? What should go into your dashboards, reports and forecasts? We covered this earlier in the section on KPIs. This is where they become super useful.

While KPIs are unique to your business, it's worth taking a moment to consider dashboard and report layout, or how desired information is displayed for ready consumption. I'll revisit an important idea here, 'at a glance'.

'At a glance' is an operational concept that simply states that in order to be useful, a dashboard should contain just enough information and be laid out in a way that it can be understood very quickly, or 'at a glance'. Good dashboards emphasise the use of graphical elements such as gauges, pie charts or simple numerical displays with clear Red / Amber / Green designations to indicate operational health or alarm conditions. Task aware and business aware software does this kind of thing straight out of the box but you should not be constrained by the ready built dashboards available to you.

If you go back to the list of questions immediately above, ask yourself what information you would need to answer them in the context of your business and take appropriate action.

That's a pretty good guide to understanding your reporting requirements. Those questions are of course not exhaustive, and you will without doubt have others that apply specifically to what you do or how you do it but the principle is the same.

To close out this section, let's consider again our friends from the introduction on their way to their school reunion. Their journey would have been infinitely easier if they'd had a GPS or Sat Nav instead of having to rely on a paper map. In the same way that a GPS will not just provide you with relevant, up to date journey information, it also keeps you up to date with all you need to know about your destination and when you'll get there.

Your management reporting capability is your GPS. All you have to do is follow it. I can't guarantee it'll be a fun ride but knowing where you are and how you'll reach your journey's end will make it as relaxing as possible.

AI AS A MANAGEMENT TOOL

At this point, a few words on AI are probably appropriate.

At the time of writing, the advent of AI tools in business is the hottest of hot topics, and much opinion is being shared on its likely impact and whether that impact will be net negative or net positive. What interests me, and in keeping with the objective of this book, is how to make AI useful to business leaders. What is AI good at that we could use to improve business performance?

A promising option is around reporting tools. AI is proving exceptionally good at collating large amounts of unrelated information and teasing out relationships between values where none might have been expected. Right now you can invest in AI based reporting software that will aggregate information from right across your organisation and present it back to you, summarised in interesting and useful ways. There is every prospect that it will even be able to identify KPIs for you that you might not have spotted for yourself.

While I encourage you to explore everything that AI tools can bring to your business, does this mean that you can completely delegate your reporting to some software? Are you off the hook when it comes to working out how best to measure business performance to make better forecasts?

As you have almost certainly guessed, no. I mean, you could, to the extent that there's nothing stopping you. But let me ask you, would you also delegate the leadership of your business to software?

That's a crazy idea, right? Handing over the visionary, inspirational role that brought this business to life? Unthinkable! But it highlights an absolutely fundamental point, which is; where does responsibility truly lie? If, as a leader you have ultimate authority to guide the business as you see fit, that must mean that ultimate responsibility must lie with you as well. Per President Harry S. Truman, "the buck stops here". If bad decisions led to bad outcomes, just pointing to your AI reporting tool and saying 'well our reporting was poor' would not be much of an excuse. So simply investing in AI reporting and hoping for the best is not effective management.

To go back to the introduction to this book and our intrepid travellers, we used the example of what can happen to an objective when you don't have accurate, timely information, and the point was made that a Sat Nav or GPS would have solved that problem right away. While that is absolutely true, it's only true if you have decided where you want to go. While a GPS can show you an optimised route to get to absolutely anywhere, as far as the machine is concerned there is no special value to that destination. In other words, it's up to you to decide where you want to end up, the machine can't decide for you.

IT & HARDWARE

We've spent some time exploring an interesting hierarchy to support the growth of our businesses. To recap:

Your business plan is a set of decisions, based on assumptions backed up by data. Your data is created as a function of your business processes, and your processes live in software.

However, software can't exist on its own. It needs something to run on.

The last requirement is hardware. The stuff everybody thinks of when they think about IT, i.e. computers and networks and internet connections and so on.

Now I promised you at the start of this book that I would only go as far into the technical realm as absolutely necessary and no further, and I'm not about to break that promise.

Let's proceed with another automotive metaphor.

Imagine a Formula 1 team setting out to win a race. What do they need for success?

A race strategy, a fast driver, a quick engine, an efficient pit crew and many other essential requirements. However none of that will make any difference to the race outcome without the very best tyres they can get their hands on.

While the team director may be primarily focused on race strategy and beating the competition, he or she will absolutely know that any weak point in race preparation will mean a loss, regardless of how well resourced the rest of the team is. While they may delegate tyre supply to a team member, they never forget that delegation does not take away their responsibility for the team's performance and the race outcome.

You can think of your IT infrastructure as your race tyres. It must be high quality and work flawlessly, otherwise everything else you do will be wasted effort.

There are two critically important points here:

- Only having most of what you need to win is the same as having none of it.
- Making sure you have everything you need to win is a management function and can't be delegated.

So while it's natural to focus on the higher levels of our information hierarchy on the basis of operational or management benefit, a business owner or leader is absolutely responsible for all of it.

So what does our busy, non technical business leader need to know about IT in order to manage it effectively? Well, let's begin with what it's supposed to do for the business. In The Productive Hour we looked at how digital tools made your people more effective and that's a fine place to start. Since most of those tools are accessed on a computer, let's consider the humble desktop PC.

There are two attributes that any PC must have in order for it to be useful. Firstly it must be fast enough that any calculation or computation it needs to do is perceived as instant. Nothing less will do. Beyond the obvious productivity benefits, there's a hidden additional reason why perceived speed is so important. If a PC is felt to be running slowly, the end user will likely have no idea why that's happening. They don't know whether it's a PC problem something to do with the rest of the IT system, or indeed whether it's something they've done wrong. The problem here is that this undermines their belief that the IT system, be it tiny or gigantic, is truly fit for purpose.

Once that doubt starts to work its way in, it can lead to all manner of other doubts. After all, if the IT system behaves strangely, does that mean the people who installed it don't know what they're doing? Or that they're just too tight fisted to buy the right equipment? If either of those statements is felt to be true, then the lid is firmly lifted on what else might not be fully understood or budgeted, and the list of possible candidates is long and depressing.

Next, any computer needs to have enough screen space to display all the required information for a given task such that it can all be seen easily and at the same time. Yes, it's possible to have multiple programs running at once on a laptop with a 14" screen, but if that person needs to consume, compare or otherwise work with all of them, then they're going to spend a lot of time bringing one program and then another to the front to actually do anything. This isn't just slow, it's also massively frustrating for the user and makes them prone to errors.

If the typical volume of information someone needs to work with can't be displayed on one screen, provide two. If it can't be displayed on two, make sure they have three. If you do an internet image search for 'stock trading workstation', you'll see what I mean. Typically these will have enough (six or even eight is not uncommon) screens to enable a highly paid expert make accurate decisions quickly. In other words, these are not in any sense a luxury, they are simply an appropriate set of tools to get the job done.

Remember, we have already shown that the capital cost of these items is a tiny fraction of the value of the business they help you transact over their lifetime.

There's something else very important to take on board here. We've just been contemplating office computers, and not once did we need to think about any of the technical aspects i.e. how many gigawobbles and thrundlenicks and flange nuggets they need and so on. All we've done is define the benefit we want from them. The beauty here is that this benefit is defined in the language of business and not the language of technology.

In other words, you could go to your technology partner using these benefits as requirements and hold them responsible for the outcome. If your team come to you complaining about their computers running slowly for example (and can demonstrate that to your satisfaction of course!) then the discussion you need to have with your tech supplier becomes simple.

You told them what you needed your computers to do, and you paid for a solution they warranted would meet your needs. If said solution subsequently falls short of expectations, it's down to them to either remedy the situation or explain in non technical language what has changed.

If you've ever been quoted for computers based on their technical specification and left to wonder whether they are really the right tool for the job, you will probably be able to see the advantage here.

While we're on the topic of desktop computers, it's worth looking at the tradeoff between budget and business value.

One of the biggest headaches for the non technical IT budget holder, is understanding why similar looking computers can cost wildly different amounts. After all, they seem to have similar components and run similar looking operating systems and software. Is a cheap one better or worse value than an expensive one?

I'm going to make one assumption at this point to keep the topic under control. The assumption is that you have a workable relationship with a technology provider and some degree of trust that their markup is reasonable. Obviously that may not be the case but as I keep reminding you, having a technology partner is a good thing in business! So let's suppose you have placed your requirements in front of your technology partner, and they give you a selection of differently priced options that they say will meet your needs. Which one to pick?

Here's one way to look at it.

If there's one characteristic that defines IT hardware in business, it's probably 'feels like it's become obsolete in about 20 minutes' i.e. as soon as you have made a hardware investment, it's time to think about its replacement.

Before we explore perception that further, it would be worth running a quick survey on the computers you already own. If you're anything like a lot of the businesses I have spoken to, you'll find that the hardware you own is actually quite a bit older than you thought it was. You shouldn't find this surprising, it frequently happens with songs you remember from the radio and your relatives ages too!

However, let's consider the obsolescence issue. I'm going to borrow another metaphor from the automotive world. Let's suppose you need to buy a car that can be driven at 70 mph. You chose 70 as your specification as that's the national speed limit and you won't ever want to go faster. You're offered two cars to choose from, one with an absolute max speed of 70 mph and another much more expensive one that could reach 100 mph or more.

Now let me ask you, which of these is likely to be nicer to drive? The one that is going absolutely flat out at 70, every panel shaking and every moving part on the verge of failure, or the theoretically faster car that is a joy to drive at 70 because it's so far from its limits?

Let's develop this further. Suppose that as your car gets older and its mechanical components start to wear out, its top speed diminishes by 5% per year. After only a couple of years, the cheaper option with the original 70 mph top speed will only be capable of about 62 mph, while the pricier option is still easily capable of running at 70.

There is some similarity between this model and the process of buying computers for your business. Although computers don't have quite as many moving parts as a car, there is a degree to which they slow down over time. While in theory both a cheap computer and an expensive one could probably support your computing workload on the day you buy it, the expensive one will stay useful in the business much longer. So you can look at spending more on a given computer as deferring the point of obsolescence and therefore replacement.

I should emphasise that this is a gross simplification, and there are many other differences between a cheap computer and an expensive one. I won't go into much more detail on this but I do want to make one last point.

Computers purpose built for business are designed with a couple of extra requirements in mind by the manufacturer. Firstly, they are expected to run all day every day, and their components and construction are chosen with this workload in mind. Additionally, they are built to be easy to fix. With the best will in the world, failures do occur and it's in everybody's interest that a fix can be completed efficiently. If a PC is constructed such that its parts are easy to access and therefore replace, then a service engineer will be able to get it back up and running quickly to both their delight and the user's!

Now that's fine and there are clear efficiency benefits to be gained from this kind of construction. But, and yes you guessed it, it comes at a cost. Purpose built business computers are just more expensive. The fact that there's an overall net benefit doesn't change the fact that the upfront price is going to be higher.

What else should you be aware of when it comes to IT hardware? As we've already seen, important business issues arise just from considering the simplest desktop PC. Could there be other examples from elsewhere in the IT domain that deserve the same level of attention?

Of course there are! Let's continue.

We need to wind the clock back a few years, and briefly review how the IT function used to support business and then compare it to today's methods.

It's important to understand that even though technology has changed out of all recognition, the objectives of the business IT function has not. People need to be able to create, store and share information in order to carry out their work. It's the task of the IT team (whether internal or external) to make sure that this happens reliably.

As it turns out, the biggest difference between then and now is geography. Only a few years ago, the work people did could almost be defined by where they did it as much as what it was. Work, or at least work with a meaningful amount of information management, happened in offices, factories and shops. What this meant was that, by accident, a geographical boundary could be placed around work. Work was the thing that happened in this building, and anything outside could be ignored from an IT point of view.

This world view, although entirely reasonable, ended up have a big impact on how IT systems were implemented. Good examples can be found in any 1980s movie where hacking is part of the plot.

Dialogue such as "They've hacked the firewall" "They're in" "They've locked me out" and similarly cheesy examples are common in these types of films, but the model they are referring to is a classic example of ' the good guys are in here, the bad guys out there'. OK, so what? Well, when all your assets are located in a single building, then you're going to need a solution to house and protect them and manage peoples access.

These were the operational conditions that gave rise to the business server.

THE BUSINESS SERVER

It's important to keep in mind that a server has several business critical jobs to do, regardless of whether it's a single machine or more than one. It typically needs to:

- Manage how networked computers talk to each other in an organised manner
- Keep a list of everyone who is authorised to use the network together with what they are allowed to see and what they are not
- Provide a safe storage place for business information
- Provide a messaging system such as email
- Host a centralised business management software solution

Without going into technical detail, you can see these tasks live at the core of the business, which means they must be carried out 24/7 with the absolute minimum risk of failure and downtime. This in turn means that servers tend to be very expensive devices indeed, and in case you thought that sounded a bit frightening, it gets worse.

How expensive I hear you ask? Well, while the short answer is 'very', the slightly longer answer is as follows. When you try to estimate how much raw computing power and data storage space you need, this must be done in the context of the expected lifespan of the server itself. If you want your server to last, by which I mean still be useful in a business sense, for say five years then you need to do some fairly serious crystal ball gazing. What is your business likely to be doing in five years? How many people will it employ? What activities will it be undertaking? How much data will it need to store and so on. The gritty reality is these questions relate to the furthest reaches of your business plan and so can't be answered in that time frame except in vague terms. From an IT planning perspective, a good guess is about the best you're going to be able to achieve.

If you don't know what your computing requirements are going to be in the expected lifespan of this machine, your only option is to play it safe. In other words, you pretty much need to specify an over powered machine as a hedge against future bets you haven't made yet. Hence an elevated price tag for today's computing requirements.

A large, powerful computer takes a fair amount of electricity to run which has its own price tag. It has to run 24/7 to allow background and housekeeping tasks to take place in quiet periods so the power bill just keeps climbing. But that's it right? We have bought our server and paid the power bill, we're off to the races now?

Whoops!

Think back a moment. This is a large, high powered computer, consuming a lot of electricity. How much heat do you think that's going to generate? You guessed it, quite a lot. Servers run best in an air conditioned environment, partly to keep them cool and partly to prevent dust accumulating inside the case. Dust is not a cosmetic issue, it tends to accumulate in fans and around other parts, preventing air flow which in turn leads to heat related outages. What does an air conditioning system need to run? Yup, more electricity.

While we're considering these additional factors, I should add that servers are typically very noisy, so this air conditioned environment needs to be away from people. And just to complete our laundry list of technical misery, our air conditioned, dust sealed, noise separated environment really needs to be locked as well. In a world where a single virus infected USB key in the wrong place can bring down an entire network, controlling physical access to a sensitive device like a server makes sense.

On the upside, servers are quite happy working in the dark, so you can save a bit by turning the lights out. As upsides go, it's not great but it's about all we've got.

So you can see that while servers are a workable solution to what were novel challenges at the dawn of networked business IT, there are built in overheads we'd like to get rid of if we could.

I wanted to go into that much depth because it's time to compare the way things were with today's business world.

The biggest change in recent years in how business IT is consumed is that geography no longer has much of a role in information management.

Hang on, what?

Simply put, the recent widespread adoption of working from home has become the most visible example of a general trend, remote working. Remote working has both driven the adoption of, and benefited from the availability of cloud services and software. I'll break that down a little.

Although remote working has been a thing for many years, because the technology it needed was a bit clunky, its use was restricted to people whose work was by definition not office based. For example sales teams and field service engineers all need to be able to create and consume up to date information to complete their work. Traditionally, this meant finding some way of connecting them temporarily back to the main office since that's where all the data lived. Dialup or VPN connections were the only possible connection options, but they worked well enough to meet the needs of the limited proportion of people that needed them.

What this model highlights is that having all your information in one place is a bit of a bottleneck. Making different sets of rules or providing different facilities for people to do their work depending on where they are creates a lot of additional complexity. In principle, it would be a lot easier for everyone involved if data was available everywhere instead of one place.

The other major change in business computing in recent years has been the migration of traditional server roles to the cloud. We looked earlier at the tasks that a server typically has to carry out on behalf of the business. What software like Microsoft 365 and Google Workspace has brought to the party is the ability to run most of those services in the cloud.

A word on cloud computing might be in order here. Simply put, cloud computing is the same as any other kind of computing, but it's provided as a service. Someone else has taken on the overheads of server ownership and is happy to provide shared access to its capabilities on a subscription basis. While there are as many different kinds of cloud services as there are businesses to consume them, the principle is the same every time.

What this has led to is a business computing environment where data is available everywhere to teams who are already used to working wherever they are. While the technology requirements for managing remote teams is outside the scope of this book, from a productivity point of view, this is a huge step forward.

Before we go on, it's worth revisiting a couple of important points raised earlier in this book. We'll begin with the criticality of your business data and ensuring its protection.

Back in the days before cloud computing, your computers and your data all lived inside your office network, which in turn was protected from the bad guys by the network firewall. At least in theory, the firewall was the only way information could get in or out of the network. While that seems like a highly controllable and therefore safe environment, there are a few not so obvious problems. To begin with, there are many ways data can be stolen, from simple printouts to USB keys right down to picking up a PC and walking out with it. If your attention is mainly focused on the integrity of the firewall, then you are likely to miss other ways that your data can be compromised.

In addition, if a network firewall completely prevents any data getting in or out, then it's not much use. After all, you want your email to be able to reach the internet, right? So while the perception is that the firewall is some impenetrable barrier to data traffic, in reality it has a number of holes in it to allow desirable traffic in and out. The tricky bit is that the behaviour of those holes, i.e. how they decide what's allowable and what isn't, is described by a set of rules and each hole has its own rule set. That's fine, but who is going to write those rules? Whoever it is had better understand every possible interpretation of every possible rule, otherwise there might be some combination of attack conditions that fall outside the expected scope of normal working but inside the limits of a given rule set. What all of this is getting at is that while a firewall is an absolute requirement to protect a business network from the internet, relying on it for the totality of your data security is not advisable.

So if your data isn't secure inside a network you own, protected by a firewall you have some control over, then isn't it even more exposed if it's stored in some third party facility on the internet where anyone can try to get at it?

Well yes, but in real terms, no.

You see, the most significant difference between your office network and an internet based could service provider is one of scale. Because of their sheer size, cloud service providers can afford to employ the very best cyber security engineers to protect their networks. So while your vital data is theoretically open to attack by anyone with an internet connection, in practice its vulnerability is more defined by your own security policies and less by limitations in the cloud provider's systems. If you ignore basic security hygiene such as complex, single use passwords, multi factor authentication and similar steps, then your data will probably be stolen regardless of how secure your cloud provider is. I would direct you back to the section on cyber security certification for guidance.

This has been a long, but necessarily long way to explain a simple but profound point. The days of needing a server in your business by default are gone.

There are exceptions of course, but not many.

Moving server activity to the cloud relies on having a high quality internet connections wherever your people are working. If your business is in a rural area with poor internet coverage then this may be more of an issue than for a city based business. We'll look at internet connections in more depth shortly, but suffice to say it's critical to take into account when thinking about cloud services.

The other notable exception is where your main line of business software can only be hosted on a server. Most business software vendors have already realised that their business model works rather better when their software is implemented in the cloud, but not all. Some still insist on having a dedicated server, with the attendant local overheads we already know about. While I can't advise you on whether it's worth migrating to a cloud based alternative due to the number of variables involved, I'd certainly suggest exploring your options.

Since it's just been highlighted as a critical component, let's examine internet connections.

INTERNET CONNECTIONS

As promised, I'm not going to spend very much time on the technology involved here, I'm only going to consider the business impacts and implications. We'll start from the assumption that you have one or more internet connection options on offer. What are the important factors for the budget holder to take into account?

- Speed
- Symmetry
- Contention
- SLA
- Failover

Speed - OK this one is obvious at a surface level, however the advertised speed of an internet link doesn't actually mean a lot on its own. Its significance comes in relation to the volume of traffic it's expected to carry. To illustrate, if you have an office with 5 people in it, you can imagine their internet traffic requirements will be lower than an office with 50 people in it. Then again, an office with 5 people whose role requires them to frequently send and receive huge data files might actually need a faster connection than 50 people just sending an occasional email.

So how fast is fast enough? Well speed can't really be considered on its own, it's just one aspect of how an internet connection behaves.

Symmetry - this is the degree to which traffic coming down from the internet has a different speed to that going up. It's worth taking a moment to understand why these speeds might be different and what that means for your business.

The legacy solution for high speed internet worked on two observations. This was that it took longer for internet content to be consumed (i.e. web pages to be read) than delivered, and that a computer's requests for web pages were very small compared to the content in the page itself. What these two very accurate observations showed, was that an internet connection that was equally fast in upload (request) and download (delivery) directions was going to be massively wasteful as most of the upload capacity would not be used. Tiny and infrequent page requests would be allocated as much bandwidth as huge and regular page downloads. Hence the development of the first broadband technology, ADSL. It many not be much of a surprise to learn that the A in ADSL stands for Asymmetric. If you've ever wondered why broadband is frequently advertised in terms of its download speed only when two very different ones are involved, it's because big numbers sound better!

So problem solved, right? If consuming data takes much longer than requesting and delivering it, then having an asymmetric connection is the perfect solution. Well yes, but it turns out that that's a hell of an 'if'. In business it's quite common to want to send large files rather than just receive them. In that instance, our asymmetric connection is trying to work backwards, i.e. using its thin upload capacity to send our huge files. In those circumstances, an asymmetric connection is a nightmare. Even though you're paying for a high speed service, most of that capacity is not being used and your team will believe that their internet connection is awful.

What's the solution here? You'll probably have guessed it's symmetrical services. In other words, an internet connection where the download speed and the upload speed are the same.

Now while this sounds simple in principle, the technical underpinnings for providing such symmetrical services are actually very different to those needed for more common kinds of internet connection. Since different technology is needed, and these services are only of benefit to a limited number of customers, they tend to be very expensive in comparison. You may know them as leased lines or similar, and while their associated price is indeed quite high, they have other attributes that add a lot of value to a business customer. More on this shortly.

There's one last technical factor and one operational one to take into account before we summarise.

Contention - this is the degree to which your internet bandwidth is shared with other users.

If you've been working from home recently, and noticed that your internet connection seems pretty zippy only to slow down in the early evening, you're probably experiencing contention in action.

Again, a few words of explanation are needed here. The principle of internet traffic being spiky or busy one moment and then quiet the next turns out to be pretty much universal. While it's possible to make quite accurate observations about internet traffic on average, those averages don't apply to individual users and specific moments in time. In other words, while an internet provider can say that a typical user or will consume x amount of bandwidth over a month or a year, there is actually no such thing as a typical user. Everyone's needs and usage patterns are different.

Why does this matter? Because the cost of providing internet access is actually very high. The amount of equipment and people required is substantial, and there is huge competitive pressure to keep end user prices as low as possible. The way around this is to leverage these known averages by sharing internet bandwidth between a number of customers. The way it works is this; if it's known that on average a user will use 10 Mb/s of bandwidth (don't worry about what those numbers actually mean, for our purposes it's ratios that are important) it doesn't mean that they will be downloading 10 Mb/s all the time. More likely they peak download demand will be 50Mb/s but most of the time their demand is actually zero. So in principle, if that user was allocated a 50 Mb/s connection and it was shared with 5 other people, then on average their internet needs will be met.

This sharing of bandwidth between multiple customers is called contention, and the number of customers sharing a single bandwidth allocation is known as the contention ratio.

So far, so good. However, we've uncovered something important here. The cost of providing a 50Mb/s connection now varies with the number of users it's shared between and that number is under the control of the internet provider. I'm sure you can see where this is going. If they share the same amount of bandwidth between a greater number of users but charge them the same amount each, they'll make more profit! Bonanza!

All of the above explains why your home internet connection seems to slow down in the evening. You'll be sharing that bandwidth with a number of other households, most of whom are out at work during the day but want their Netflix etc. in the evening. A domestic internet service might have a contention ration of 50:1 or each customer shares their bandwidth with 49 others. While that might seem ridiculously high, it works well enough for internet providers to be able to offer their services at an affordable price.

OK, now we understand the principle, how does it apply to our businesses?

Well this is where the different demand characteristics of business start to kick in. While a slow internet connection at home might be aggravating, during the day when you need to be at your most responsive to customers it's a legitimate crisis. You absolutely cannot afford to have your internet performance impact by the demands of other businesses, particularly since they can't be estimated.

So what to do? Well as you might imagine, your friendly local internet provider has already thought of that. They will happily offer you a 'business' internet connection, which is the same as a domestic one in all respects except it has a lower contention ratio. If domestic services were provided on a ratio of say 50:1, business services might have a ratio of 20:1. Note that nothing else has changed, but on average your internet connection will seem faster just because it is shared with fewer others. This is important because there is no guarantee that this average will influence the connection to the same degree at all times. If another customer is seriously hammering their own connection for an extended period, yours might still suffer. Equally, the reverse is true. Exceptionally heavy internet use by your company might affect another. Please keep in mind that whichever way round this happens, the heavy user may not be aware of the impacts they are having, nor will anyone else affected know who is causing the issue. There's no way round this, it's just the way the system works.

If any kind of contention seems like an unacceptable compromise to you, again you have options. The symmetrical leased line service mentioned earlier had another upside - dedicated bandwidth. Leased line services are completely reserved for you, you can use them at full capacity 24/7 if you wish. While these services sometimes seem unreasonably expensive, they have advantages that other services just can't match.

OK, that's the technical stuff out of the way. We need to include one more factor in our list of variables that affect internet connection choice. It's Service Level Agreement or SLA.

When you take a service from a provider, it will have some description of what's being provided and under what terms or conditions. These might be tightly defined or not, but combined they form a service level. For example, if the service fails, what is the provider required to do to fix it? This could be anything from 'it'll be fixed inside a certain time' down to 'nothing we can do, sorry'. As business users, it's in our interest to understand what service level is offered and whether it meets our needs. Bear in mind, our needs in this case will be defined in the context of worst case scenario, i.e. there's been some catastrophic failure somewhere and we need concrete guarantees to fall back on to help us plan our recovery.

So if that's a service level, how do we make sure it's observed by the provider? That's where a formal agreement is required, known as a Service Level Agreement. An SLA is (usually) offered by the service provider and agreed in a formal way by both the provider and you, the customer. It could contain elements such as:

- Response metrics in case of failure (first response to alert, customer update frequency etc.)
- Minimum fix time, time to site for an engineer
- Penalties or service credits in case of SLA breach

An SLA is a subtle and complex beast and despite being used to describe a technical service, is written in legal language. In case that sounds daunting, an SLA is huge advantage for a business customer such as you. It enables you to put some reliable statements around your own business recovery plans in the event of bad things happening. This is particularly important if you have your own service agreements with your customers which could be impacted by an internet outage.

OK it's time to sum up. What have we covered in the context of internet services?

We know that connection speed on its own it not a good guide to suitability for your business. You also need to understand what your user requirements are for each location you're considering.

Do you need a symmetrical internet service with its corresponding price tag? Is it worth paying for a leased line simply to enjoy the benefits of an SLA?

What contention ratio are you prepared accept? If price is a major factor for you, then you may have to acknowledge that internet performance may vary unpredictably and make operational allowances around this.

Once again, you are not entirely on your own here. Your technology support partner can advise on how best to meet your unique requirements. However, as a business leader, the final choice rests with you together with its implications.

Let's assume that you have taken all the above aspects into account, and made your choice regarding your internet connection. You have enjoyed the benefits of your dazzlingly informed decision making for some period, but all of a sudden your internet connection goes down. What now? Your users may have ground to a halt, and you have become invisible to your customers, suppliers and partners. While you reach for whatever service level you were offered or agreed, you may be thinking "wouldn't it be great to have a spare connection right about now?"

Yes. Yes it would.

As your reliance on internet based services increases, the negative impacts of losing them are only going to become greater. On that basis, some thought should be given to reserve capacity to protect against such failures. What you want is some solution that sits in the background, such that when your main connection fails, it can 'fail over' to your reserve one. Hence these services are commonly referred to as failover solutions.

Failover solutions come in a number of different flavours, and again it's down to you as a business leader to make a choice. Let's look at some options.

More of same - if you have one kind of connection service, you could in theory just order another one and arrange things so that when one service fails the other one is ready to take over. While that's fine in principle, it does mean that you are in effect only using half the combined service you are paying for. It's also worth keeping in mind that having identical main and failover services leaves you exposed to common effects. For example, if you got both services from the same provider and they experienced a significant technical failure, then potentially both your main and failover links could die at the same time.

Even if you tried to play it safe and bought services from different providers, there are still common factors. Think for a moment how the cables or fibres actually reach your building. They are typically delivered through underground pits and ducts, and since each building is usually only supplied from a single duct, it's plausible that some interruption like a some crazed digger driver going through it through sheer carelessness would cut both cables and take both services out at the same time.

So if identical duplicate services are considered too risky, what about non identical? For example, if your main connection was supplied over optical fibre, what about using 4G or 5G mobile broadband for failover purposes? While this is technically perfectly feasible, it does depend on the availability of a sufficiently high strength mobile signal in your location. You may also need to mount some kind of outdoor antenna if mobile reception turns out to be a bit iffy indoors. If you don't own the building you're operating from, what permissions would you need to do this and can they even be granted?

Let's suppose you have found some sufficiently reliable, affordable way of protecting the vital internet connection into your main building. Bingo! Problem solved, drinks all round! But hang on, who's not lifting a celebratory glass with you? That's right, everyone who's out on the road or working from home or some other remote location. Remember, their value to the business is measured in what they're doing not where they are. Having invested in cloud computing solutions so your people can be effective regardless of location, their individual connections to the internet are arguably as important as a main office one.

How are you going to protect everyone's separate internet connections? Is that option even affordable? If not, what operational solution are you going to put in place to manage the impact of individual connection failures? Will your people need to come into a main office? Is there even a main office to come into? You can see that while aspects of this planning are technical, the most important parts are operational, i.e. pure management responsibility.

So to close out our section on IT infrastructure and services, what have we learned?

First and foremost, although the technologies underlying your business do not need to be understood in depth by a business leader, their importance and impacts absolutely must be. The what and the how can be delegated to your technical experts, but the why has real management significance and cannot be ignored.

SUPPORT SERVICES

Having spent time looking at your physical IT infrastructure and the enabling role it plays in all other aspect of information handling in your business, you can see that making sure it's as reliable as it can be is crucial. We have shown the negative impacts of IT outages, right down to the cash value per hour. On that basis, it is clearly critically important that you have an effective technology support function in place.

We're going to look at different ways that can be achieved, and why some are surprisingly less effective than they might seem at first glance.

Broadly speaking, your support options are as follows:

- Don't bother. Nothing's gone wrong so far so it probably won't.
- One of our team is good at computers. They fix things when needed.
- We know a computer expert. They will come out when we need them.
- We have a support supplier and a comprehensive service plan.
- We have a technology partner for the business.
- We have an in house IT team

Looking at them in turn.

WE DON'T BOTHER WITH IT SUPPORT

Modern technology is pretty reliable, and we only bought these computers recently so they ought to run for the foreseeable without breaking.

Although you can already see how this apparently reasonable argument might come apart on you at the worst possible time, it's worth taking a moment to examine the business mindset in play here. Once again, you'll remember we've examined how businesses start, and in particular the cash constraints they start under. While the excitement level is high, this is a tricky time to be peering into the future and trying to estimate what costs enterprise will need to bear at some indeterminate point to come. Sure you have a plan for growth, but today and tomorrow it's not clear how accurate that plan is. After all, the volume of data you have to work with to validate all your starting assumptions is low, so as we have already seen your plan is broadly speaking a set of guesses and will remain so until you have better data to work with. If it's not clear what your income position will be, it's tricky to know what costs you can afford.

While this view of the world is understandable, and may even get you through the early days of trading, it's very much a ticking timebomb. The point of view that because nothing has gone wrong yet, it won't in the future is not a good one and will let you down at some point. The problem is, the longer it takes for some serious issue to arise, the stronger your faith in the original thinking becomes. The quid pro quo is that the longer it takes for some serious outage to occur, the worse the impact will be. By definition, you will be least prepared for something you don't think will happen! The important point in this situation is to recognise that it is unsustainable in the longer term and to investigate better alternatives quickly.

WE HAVE RACHEL OR MALCOLM IN OUR TEAM.

They know about computers and can fix them when they go wrong.

At a surface level, this looks like a good tradeoff between cost and utility. In fact it's nothing of the kind but we need to dig down a little to understand why.

Let's examine what happens in a simplified fault situation. Somebody's PC starts doing something weird or stops working completely. The call for help goes out, and Rachel heads over to start investigating the problem. In this example the affected user is in the same building so Rachel doesn't have far to travel and she can start working on the fault straight away. While that may seem fine, it's ignoring a couple of important factors.

To begin with, the fault has stopped our first team member from working. You'll recall from the section on The Productive Hour that this is not cost free. There is both a cost per hour and a value per hour attached to that person's time, and right now we're looking at the downside of both. But wait, it gets worse. Remember, Rachel is not solely employed in an IT support role, she has her own work with its attached cost and value. So, to help someone else with their IT fault, she has had to stop her own work. This means that we now have two unproductive people, not one.

Suppose you accept this solution as a price worth paying.

After all, how long can it take someone to fix a PC? Our productivity hit can't be that long, right? Then we're back to business as usual.

The problem is, the 'time to fix a fault' issue is extremely unpredictable, particularly in this operational scenario. You see, while it's possible that a fault might arise entirely within and remain limited to a single PC, it's rather more likely that there are network based factors involved. After all, as we already know, a PC isn't much use on its own and we expect it to be able work with many others to share data etc. The processes by which this is managed are massively more complex than those happening purely inside one computer.

This leaves poor Rachel with the prospect of trying to fix a fault that was reported as a single PC going wrong (with corresponding expectations of a rapid fix) which may actually be substantially more difficult to resolve. Keep in mind, while Rachel may have gained worthwhile skills with individual computers as an interest or hobby, since her role is not primarily IT focused, her opportunities to work with industrial networks of computers will obviously be more limited. The outcome is that she will suddenly find her skills not equal to the task she is presented with, which itself is already an emergency.

Poor Rachel. She's doing her best, but she's been put in an unsupportable position by her management team who are relying on unsafe assumptions to ensure the continuity of their IT systems.

So if a partial 'in house' resource is not the answer to IT support due to limited experience, surely there are people who offer the necessary skills when needed. Why not give one of them a call when something goes wrong? Again, this looks good at a surface level but there are downsides that need a little investigation.

CALL AN IT ENGINEER

Let's assume some kind of IT fault has occurred in your business and you want to hire an engineer to come and fix it. A little research delivers 5 phone numbers for IT engineers within a 25 mile radius. So all you need to do is call one, describe the fault, wait for them to come over and you're back up and running, right?

Not quite. There are a few built in assumptions here that don't bear much scrutiny.

Remember, you're not an IT expert yourself, so you have no way of being able to tell whether anyone you're talking to really knows what they're doing or just sounds convincing. Let's suppose you ask a business colleague who they have used or might recommend. Fine in principle, however since they also are not technology experts, their past experience may not be a good guide to your future one. Suppose you find that the only engineer with any references has a few outstanding references plus another one that's so bad that actual violence was contemplated. In other words, how are you going to decide which is the best engineer for you?

Moving on, let's assume you now have the phone number of an IT engineer who you are happy knows their stuff and you want to come out to look at your IT issue that has already cost you several hours productivity. You call Edwin and explain the problem as best you can. "Fine" he says, "I'll be there on Tuesday afternoon". Since it's now Thursday morning, this is probably not what you want to hear. Edwin goes on to explain that since he widely recommended he is in demand, which means he is already booked up until next week.

For the sake of our example, let's roll the clock forward to the following Tuesday and Edwin's arrival.

The good news is that Edwin is indeed a competent IT engineer, and equal to the task of fixing whatever has gone wrong. Great news, right? The cost clock is still ticking and you're already into way more downtime than you anticipated. So Edwin gets started. His first task is to assess the fault, but as have already seen for poor Rachel a PC fault is just as likely to be network related as it is to be confined to that one machine. This means that Edwin, skilled though he is, is starting from scratch in terms of understanding how your network is configured and he needs to make sure he's up to speed with this before he can gauge what kind of fault he's dealing with. Please bear in mind, you've had no professional technology support previously, which means there are likely no records and no documentation on how things have been set up. Arguably worse, you do have documentation which is now out of date. It won't be clear which parts are accurate and which aren't, so regardless Edwin is starting from the very beginning. Even if he has been to your site before, it's somewhere between possible and likely that things will have changed and even his own documentation is somewhat out of date.

OK but he has at least started, right? We're on our way to service restoration. Yes, but bear one last thing in mind. Edwin is almost certainly charging you by the hour. In case that hasn't set some mental alarm bells ringing, ask yourself what his incentive is to complete the job as quickly as possible. If, in a state of high stress, you did not respond well to his estimate of several days to get to your site (I'll leave it to your imagination what 'did not respond well' might look like and how that might have been received), do you think Edwin is highly motivated to get you back up and running as soon as physically possible?

Of course he is. Edwin is, after all, a thorough professional and really wants to get a good outcome for you the customer. However, what if you had originally spoken to his competitor Evil Edwin? Tricky times may be ahead.

So we can see that having an IT expert on speed dial is not quite the improvement it first seems. What else have we got?

How about having IT support as a service based on a known monthly payment? Why might that be better?

IT SERVICE PROVIDER

The biggest clue is in the word 'service'. As we have seen when examining internet connectivity options, a managed service is delivered according to agreed metrics which means your expectations will be based on written evidence.

However, the biggest difference between the ad hoc model we just looked at and a managed service is the operational and commercial focus of the service provider.

To explain:

Someone providing ad hoc services such as Edwin makes all their income from outages, failures and other adverse situations. Their service is based on repairing things that have broken, so it's not in their interest to prevent these kinds of events. By contrast, a managed service provider will want to support as many customers as they can within a fixed resource base, i.e. support engineers and systems. What this means is it's very much in their interest to prevent failures so their engineers spend as little time on outages or unpredictable tasks as possible. Unpredictable tasks by definition can't be planned for accurately so to accommodate them they need to resource for a worst case. The more unpredictable their task volume becomes, the more they need to over resource.

This leads to a win / win between you the customer and the IT support service provider. A reliable IT network that meets the needs of your users also represents a lucrative engagement for your support partner. What's not to like?

So if your support provider really wants your IT to be as reliable as possible, what can they do to ensure this is the outcome you get? What tricks can they bring to bear?

This is where remote monitoring and remote support step in. If you've ever worked in a large organisation with easy access to IT support, you'll know that an engineer in some other location can instantly take control of your PC and start investigating the fault. Borderline magical as that may seem, it's actually significantly more effective than that. The thing is, the degree to which you can see what's going on inside your PC from your own keyboard is actually very limited. There is a wealth of activity going on 'under the hood' which is hidden from the user. This is actually where the IT support engineer does most of their work. They have tools and techniques at their disposal which are simply not available to you at your desk, and they can apply substantial diagnostic power which you won't be aware of while its working.

It's important to draw a comparison between this scenario and poor Rachel's best efforts to fix a wayward PC. Since her employer (that's you by the way!) doesn't have expensive enterprise grade IT diagnostic tools within the business, neither does she. Her ability to diagnose and fix is restricted to whatever she can find out directly from your keyboard. It's also highlighting the difference you experienced between waiting for an engineer to come to site, and having one at the end of the phone who not only can start work immediately but is likely to have a fully detailed picture of your whole network configuration to aid them.

If this sounds pretty good, how else could a company like this help us?

How about supplying your IT hardware and software? Let's look at hardware first. We previously considered how choosing something as basic as a desktop computer was a little more subtle than it first appears. It became apparent that a cheap PC is likely to turn out to be a false economy and end up costing you more over its lifespan than a more expensive one. What if you went to your IT support provider for your computers? Would there be any benefit in doing that? Again yes, as we have seen. If your hardware supplier is also tasked and incentivised with making sure your IT systems work as expected, then they will tend to supply PCs that are both reliable and easy to fix in the event of failure.

But hang on, will these come at a price premium? Could you find them cheaper yourself? Almost certainly yes. So is there a tangible benefit in doing so? Actually, probably not. Firstly, the greater proportion of your IT infrastructure that's sourced from a single provider, the more responsibility they have for its performance. If however you are determined to pay the least amount possible for your computers, then additional overheads such as warranty admin fall to you. If you experience a PC failure that falls under the scope of warranty, then it's down to you to make that claim, arrange for return shipping, make some arrangement for a temporary machine while your new one is under repair etc. If you are costing your admin time appropriately (The Productive Hour!) then you'll see that admin costs could potentially outstrip any cash saving you might have made.

What else could they do for you? If hardware supply to complement hardware support is in scope, what about software? Are there any benefits to sourcing your software from your support provider? If the admin overhead of managing licensing is something you'd like to get rid of then yes. As your business grows and you take on more people, they're probably going to need one or more pieces of software to get their work done. You will need to make sure that you have enough licenses for everyone, and if someone leaves the business that their license is either cancelled or reallocated. If your support provider was a one stop shop for all things technical, it would remove a significant admin burden from your team.

Is this as good as it gets? Does having a support provider delivering a range of high quality services to agreed performance criteria meet all your needs?

Almost.

If nothing were ever to change, if tomorrow could be guaranteed to look like today forever, then arguably we have our perfect solution. But that's not the game we're in. Our mission is to grow the business in order to achieve the vision that started this whole enterprise in the first place. Growth equals change, so we can be sure that tomorrow will not look like today.

If your business is to grow, it's very likely that your technology needs will change along with everything else. While this is a nice problem to have, it's a problem nevertheless. How are you going to make essential strategic technology choices? How will you pick the correct software solutions and make sure they're successfully implemented?

This is where a full technology partner can step in. Acting as your senior technology adviser, they can be tasked with translating your commercial objectives into an aligned technology plan. Clearly, this kind of advisory role requires a business skill set that won't be available from every technology support provider.

If your product is exclusively promoted, sold and delivered over the internet, then tech is at the heart of everything you do and senior level guidance is essential.

There's one final example of technology support to look at.

THE IN-HOUSE TEAM

I'm going to make an assumption here, that our imaginary in house IT role is just one person. The points I'm about to make are still true for a higher number but are clearest in the case of a single support person.

Let's go back to our valiant part time engineer Rachel.

In our example earlier, Rachel was tasked with supporting the rest of her team while also being responsible for her own valuable work. We saw that this support model is deeply flawed while appearing superficially workable. So let's suppose that after a number of unsatisfactory support incidents, Rachel makes the point that she could be more effective in the support role if she was allowed to concentrate on it full time.

Again, this sounds plausible but real world implications mean it isn't. Once again, for the benefit of the example, I'm going to assume that her salary is considered to be a reasonable price for having an on demand IT support function. I'll include the cost of the various service management systems such as support ticket management software and remote monitoring systems. I'll even factor in the skills needed to get these systems up and running, which are not at all trivial.

Where have we got to? Rachel is now allowed to dedicate all her time to IT issues as they arise, and has a reasonable tool set at her disposal to help her fix them as quickly as possible. Sounds ideal, right? After all, the huge advantage here is that Rachel already knows the business and is trusted by management and the wider team. Surely this will make her extra effective?

Absolutely it will, but even that won't make up for the one huge shortfall that Rachel can do nothing about. There's only one of her.

The expectation that having an internal support resource will be able to attend to all IT issues as they arise, ignores the uncomfortable truth that these incidents don't happen on a predictable basis. In other words, you're just as likely to have 3 faults at the same time as you are to have 3 months with none at all. What this means is you are losing two ways at the same time. Rachel can't deliver the value you expect while there's nothing to fix, but also can't deliver the value you need when there are more faults than she can attend to at once.

If that seems less than ideal, keep in mind Rachel is employed for the same 40 hours per week as the rest of her team, however that 40 hours is effectively diluted by her annual leave and any sickness time she might need. What are you going to do for IT support while she's away? Fate, being the fickle beast it is, will ensure that tech failures will happen most frequently when you have no cover available. Again, the expectation is that having a full time dedicated resource is the same as having full time support cover when in fact it isn't.

What are you going to do? Employ another support person so they can cover each other's availability gaps? You could, but the costs here are starting to get very frightening, and if you think about it you have only diluted the problem not solved it.

The essential point is that your requirements have not been clarified. You don't really want people in a support role, what you actually want is guaranteed effective, reasonably priced IT support for your team at such times as they are working. If you take a step back and look at that as a service specification instead, you'll see that at the scale of small to medium business, the law of averages means internal support cannot achieve this service level. Once your business gets a lot larger, by which I mean many hundreds of employees, then your support needs will smooth out, i.e. on average faults will arise in fairly predictable volumes. At the same time, the averaged availability of a correspondingly larger internal support team should be able to deliver an appropriate service level. However, until your business reaches a substantial size, an internal IT support function makes little sense.

We have spent a long time looking at IT infrastructure and its requirements, possibly more time than you would have expected in a book about decision making. Why is this and what have we learned?

We have clearly shown that technology has no value on its own. Its sole reason for existence is as an enabling layer for businesses to manage their information to make effective decisions. However, since your technology layer supports all the other layers in the information management hierarchy, its performance and reliability are of critical business importance. We have also established that for an ambitious, growth minded business, having someone to create a technology strategy is a great advantage. Finally we understand that a technology strategy is a supporting part of your information management strategy.

On that basis, the information management role (often known as the CIO or Chief Information Officer) in your senior leadership team should always be senior to the technology lead regardless of whether the technical lead is internal or external. There are two points to make here. Firstly, even a full technology partner will still need managing, and the more strategic their input, the more senior their supervision needs to be. Secondly, that supervisory role must own the information management objectives of the business as they relate to its growth plan.

It may even be that the responsibilities of the CIO are insufficiently well understood within your management team to be executed effectively, and require an independent contractor to fulfil them. While not a cheap option, it does allow you as a business leader to concentrate on other areas of growth, in the knowledge that both your information management and technology management needs are appropriately resourced.

Finally, in case you feel I'm being overly specific here in separating the information management and technology management functions, I'm not.

Even though they are highly interrelated, they are not just different aspects of the same thing. The common misconception that they are, has led us to the mess we frequently see in business, where the wrong tools are used for information management just because that's what was available. As we now know, using the wrong tools creates huge problems and can take significant resource to fix.

SUMMARY

IN CLOSING

So we made it to the end of this book. It's been quite a journey so well done! What have we discovered thus far? Let's backtrack.

To begin with, "work on your business not in your business", while sounding somewhat trite is a surprisingly profound statement which shines a startlingly clear light on both the role and the value of the business leader and can be used as a reality check for daily activity.

While everybody's interpretation of this statement will be unique, all those interpretations can be distilled as examples of decision making.

Effective business management both relies on and derives from effective decision making. Decisions are only as good as the assumptions they are based on, and assumptions should be tested with accurate, reliable, timely business data.

Data is both created and consumed by business processes, and processes are expressed in the software tools you and your team use to carry out their given tasks. Software needs an appropriate environment to run in, i.e. the computers and networks that make up your IT system.

This hierarchy can be expressed in a single, simple diagram:

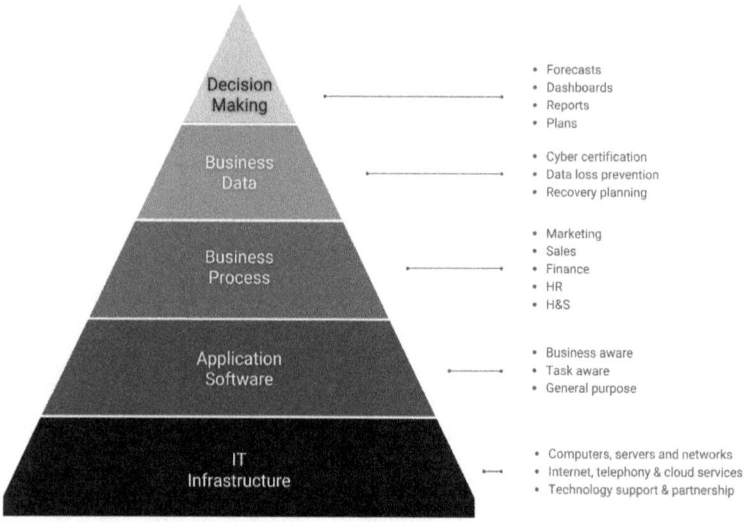

So what's next? Where do you go from here?

That depends to some extent on where you are right now.

If you are pre launch, and are still in the process of assembling your business plan, have another look at the assumptions your plan is based on. How honest have you been with yourself when defining and testing them? Wanting your assumptions to be true is perfectly understandable, but the more brutal you are in testing now, the more you will be able to rely on them when things get weird in the future.

If you are in the first couple of years of trading then now is an ideal time to review your original long term goals. To what extent are they still relevant? Has real world operating conditions revealed unexpected, possibly better ones? Does your business plan accurately reflect your business destination and your progress in getting there?

Finally, if you operate a much more mature business, then I would propose that now is a good time to reassess how decisions are really made at senior management level. Do the day to day demands of running your business distract you from making long term, complex decisions? Is your business plan a dynamic, living document or something you dust off once per year when your accountant asks to see it? Is it even relevant to your business any more?

With this last scenario in mind, but applicable to all, I wanted to close with a thought experiment.

Find your current long term growth goals, and multiply them by 10.

Yes, I really meant that, multiply by 10.

Next, try to capture what your business would look like at that scale. If it helps, write down what the org chart might look like for the larger business. How many people would you need? What would they be doing? What about space, machinery, suppliers, distributors and outlets? How much of each of these sound like enough?

Once you have been through this exercise and imagined your business massively larger than you ever have before, consider your original goals again. Do they seem a bit tame now? Does this feel like an ideal opportunity to create a new, much bolder plan?

The point I am making here, and the one I want to close with, is that ambitious, visionary decision making is not the exclusive domain of startup and early stage enterprises. You can set your sights as high as you like, and effective, evidence based decision making will get you there!

FURTHER READING

The E-Myth Revisited: Why Most Small Businesses Don't Work and What to Do About It by Gerber, Michael E.

Zero to One by Peter Thiel, Blake Masters

The Lean Startup: How Today's Entrepreneurs Use Continuous Innovation to Create

Radically Successful Businesses by Eric Ries

Our Iceberg is Melting: Changing and Succeeding Under Any Conditions by John Kotter and Holger Rathgeber

ABOUT THE AUTHOR
JONATHAN COZENS

Jonathan Cozens is a seasoned business strategist and consultant with a passion for empowering leaders to achieve sustainable growth through clear, evidence-based decision-making. Drawing on decades of experience in business management and technology, Jonathan's work bridges the gap between strategy, processes, and technology to drive meaningful results.

In his debut book, Clarity Driven, he shares practical insights and frameworks to help leaders navigate the complexities of modern business with confidence and vision. Jonathan's relatable anecdotes and accessible guidance make Clarity Driven an essential resource for leaders looking to transform challenges into opportunities.

When not writing or consulting, you'll find him exploring highways and byways on his Harley Davidson Road Glide or hard at work in the dojo training in Shotokan karate.